The Royal Court Theatre presents

the treatment

by Martin Crimp

First performance at the Royal Court Theatre on
15 April 1993

Financially assisted by the Royal Borough of Kensington and Chelsea

Recipient of an Arts Council Incentive Funding Award

Recipient of a grant from the Theatre Restoration Fund &

from the Foundation for Sports & the Arts

Registered Charity number 231242

SPRINGBOARDS

A four week celebration of new work in the Cottesloe theatre, ranging from ancient epic through music theatre to explorations of modern life.

This unique theatrical event is presented by the Royal National Theatre Studio and studio theatres nationwide.

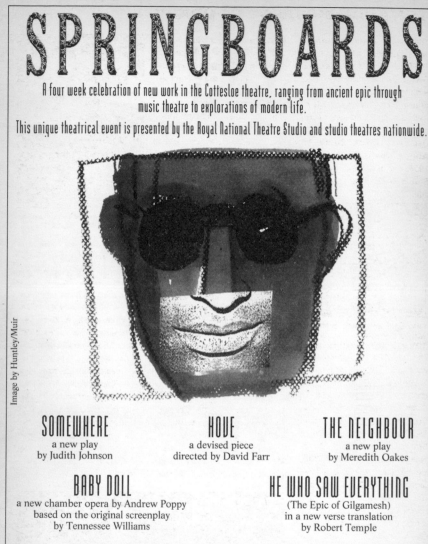

Image by Huntley/Muir

SOMEWHERE
a new play
by Judith Johnson

HOVE
a devised piece
directed by David Farr

THE NEIGHBOUR
a new play
by Meredith Oakes

BABY DOLL
a new chamber opera by Andrew Poppy
based on the original screenplay
by Tennessee Williams

HE WHO SAW EVERYTHING
(The Epic of Gilgamesh)
in a new verse translation
by Robert Temple

Springboards is supported by the John S. Cohen Foundation

For a leaflet with details of *Springboards* events at the National and in Birmingham, Edinburgh, Leicester, London, Liverpool and Salisbury, ring 071 633 0880

21 APRIL - 15 MAY 1993
Tickets: All seats £10
(restricted view £6)
Student Standby £5.50

ROYAL
NATIONAL
THEATRE

Reg'd Charity

BOX OFFICE
071-928 2252
COMPUTERISED BY
digital
C.C. WELCOME

THE ENGLISH STAGE COMPANY

The Company was formed to bring serious writing back to the stage. The Court's first Artistic Director, George Devine, encouraged new writing that explored subjects drawn from contemporary life as well as pursuing European plays and classics. When John Osborne's **Look Back In Anger** was first produced in 1956, and revived in '57, it led British theatre into the modern age.

Pamela Nomvete, Nicholas Monu & Joanne Campbell in TALKING IN TONGUES by Winsome Pinnock, 1991

The ambition to discover new work which was challenging, innovatory and also of the highest quality increasingly became the Company's artistic policy. Early Court writers included Arnold Wesker, John Arden, David Storey, Ann Jellicoe, N. F. Simpson and Edward Bond. They were followed by a generation of writers led by David Hare and Howard Brenton, and in more recent years, celebrated house writers have included Caryl Churchill, Timberlake Wertenbaker, Robert Holman and Jim Cartwright. Many of their plays are now regarded as modern classics.

In line with the policy of nurturing new writing, the Theatre Upstairs has mainly been seen as a place for exploration and experiment, where writers learn and develop their skills prior to the demands of the Main Stage auditorium. In 1991, Winsome Pinnock's **Talking in Tongues** met with both critical and popular acclaim. She has now been commissioned for the Main House. Other graduates who have moved from Upstairs to Down are Anne Devlin, Andrea Dunbar, Sarah Daniels, Jim Cartwright and Clare McIntyre. Most recently, the Theatre Upstairs has proved its value as a focal point for new work with the production of the Chilean writer Ariel Dorfman's **Death and the Maiden**. After a sell-out run in the Main House, it moved to the Duke of York's Theatre. In fact 1991 and 1992 saw record-breaking years at the box office, with **Top Girls**, **Three Birds Alighting on a Field**, **Faith Healer**, **Death and the Maiden**, **Six Degrees of Separation** (which moved to the Comedy Theatre) and **King Lear**, in 1993, all performing to near capacity. **Death and the Maiden** won the 1992 Olivier Award for Best Play. **Three**

Bill Paterson and Michael Byrne in DEATH AND THE MAIDEN by Ariel Dorfman, 1992

Birds Alighting on a Field has been awarded Best West End Play by the Writers' Guild of Great Britain, and has been successfully revived. **Six Degrees of Separation** has just been nominated the 1993 Olivier Award for Best Play.

After nearly four decades, the Royal Court Theatre is still the most important focus in the country for the production of new work. Scores of plays first seen in Sloane Square are now part of the National and International dramatic repertoire.

TOP GIRLS by Caryl Churchill, 1991

LITTLE ROMANCE - TWO EXTRACTS FROM

1) THE HOTEL STUART

It was a long time since she'd made love to a man. Would Harding know that? The stairs of the hotel twisted round and round as if they were inside a tower. On the third floor the thin carpet ended and they went up on the bare treads until they reached Harding's door. The key was attached to a huge perspex triangle with the room number embedded. He opened the door with it and made way for her. The light was on because - as she would discover - hardly any daylight reached this part of the building. A suitcase lay open on the bed. Harding walked past her, took some papers from a table, shut them into the suitcase and put the suitcase on the floor.

The only way to fit the bed into the tiny room had been to push one side of it against the wall. Harding sat on it to take off his shoes, gray sneakers which might originally have been white. He seemed to be concentrating on recovering his breath from the long climb. He'd not spoken on the stairs, and for the first time it occurred to her that perhaps she should be afraid of him. In the street he'd been gentle and surprising. In the room he was simply a man, a stranger, bending over her shoes.

He eased the sneakers off his feet with his toes and sat back on the bed, holding out his arm to her. He said "Susan?" in a startling way that almost made her look round for another person. She took off her own shoes and climbed onto the bed beside her. As she did so something tangled in her hair. She jerked her head away and raised her hand to protect herself. "It's the switch" said Harding. "Did the light-switch frighten you?" He stood up on the bed and wound the string of the pull-switch round his hand, knotting it near the ceiling, then came down again and kissed her.

Was making love something else she'd abandoned? Or had it simply been forgotten? It came from another epoch of her life, like something you might come across in a shoebox at the back of a wardrobe, like the school photograph she'd found in which she'd appeared, unbelievable, in knee-socks and a pleated skirt, almost unbearably innocent. Fucking Harding was like digging - yes digging, pushing, pushing into the past and turning up forgotten images of herself. And at the same time it was a kind of sinuous twisting, a twisting and winding, like the string in Harding's fist, mechanically climbing the stairs floor after floor, round and round until you reached light and found yourself out on the roof, right at the edge of the roof, about to scream and fall.

When she woke up the light was out, and Harding was no longer in the bed. She felt for the cord but remembered how he'd tied it out of reach. She groped her way to the door where she found the wall-switch, which was the old-fashioned kind, dome-shaped like a desk-bell with a stiff metal lever. The light seemed to eddy round the naked bulb like the heavy vapour of petrol or scent. At the foot of the bed Harding lay asleep with his head on the suitcase, his long white hair spread out on the blue leather. The light didn't wake him. He looked like a man, she thought, who could sleep anywhere, through anything.

She dressed and went out onto the stairs to find a bathroom. She headed down until the thin crimson carpet reappeared. Almost immediately a door opened and a man came out and ran down the stairs bang bang bang like a schoolboy, leaving a woman standing in the doorway.

"Excuse me" said Susan. "Is there a bathroom on this floor?"

"How d'you mean?" said the woman.

"I mean a bathroom, for guests, somewhere to wash."

"Guests?"

The woman looked at Susan. She seemed to be smiling very faintly. Finally she said, "You've nothing on your feet. Aren't you cold?"

"I need to wash."

"Why don't you wash in your room?"

"There's no water."

"You mean there are rooms without water? How d'you manage?"

"I don't know" said Susan. "I've just arrived."

"But that's a fucking disgrace" said the woman. "How can they give someone a room without water in it? Do you have a <u>toilet</u>?"

"No" said Susan. "Should there be?"

"Not even a toilet. These people make me sick - you know" - she poked two fingers into her mouth - "vomit." Then she cupped her hands like a megaphone and shouted: "YOU FUCKING MEAN BASTARDS WHY DON'T YOU GET BACK ON THE FUCKING BOAT!" Then she laughed and Susan joined in, but faintly.

"My name's Corinne" said the woman. "Why don't you come in and use mine."

"You've got a bathroom then?"

"You bet I fucking have. Come in. Jesus <u>Christ</u>."

Corinne's room was considerably larger than Harding's. There was space for a plain white table on each side of the double bed. On one of these was a bowl of fruit and on the other a large glass ashtray which Corinne emptied into a metal wastebin, printed on the outside to resemble wood. "I know I smoke too much" she said "but what I try and do is after every ten cigarettes I eat a piece of fruit. That way it kind of evens out - don't you think?"

Corinne was clearly much younger than she'd seemed in the doorway, maybe seventeen or eighteen at the most, and although she'd invited her in willingly enough, Susan's presence made her uncomfortable. Perhaps Corinne felt that she was being judged - by the room, by the ashtray full of crushed butts - even though it had already been established that at least in terms of room and facilities, she, Susan, was distinctly inferior. She wanted to start a conversation with Corinne that would set them on an equal footing, but when she said, "D'you actually live here? Is this your home?" the words came out with unmistakable condescension when she'd been striving for just the opposite, and Corinne rolled her eyes and rather than answer the question said in a false jokey way, "You call this <u>living</u>?" Then she added, as if to

WORK IN PROGRESS BY MARTIN CRIMP

shift things on. "The bathroom's through there. Didn't you bring any things?"

"What things?"

"Things like soap and things."

"No. I'm sorry. I didn't think to."

"Well that's OK" said Corinne. "I've got a load of stuff in there you can use. What kind of skin d'you have?"

"Skin?"

"I mean are you sensitive? oily? dry? What are you?"

"I don't know" said Susan.

Corinne came up to her and pushed her fingers hard into Susan's hair. It was the second time that night that someone had been so close, breathing into her face. She could see the minute jerky movements of Corinne's eyes as they examined her hairline, while the fingers dug into her scalp.

"Dry" she said. "Your skin is really dry. So is your hair."

The bathroom was not in fact a separate room. It had been made by putting up a wooden partition with glass panels near the ceiling to let in light from the room proper - since the bathroom had no light of its own. Susan crouched in the long white enamel bath to wash herself, while on the other side of the partition Corinne carried on talking.

"The Americans had a good name for them - gooks - that's a really good name for them, isn't it. Every time I see one I think to myself "gook". It's so funny and it's so right."

"What?" shouted Susan from the bath.

"The Vietnamese. They called them gooks. I love that word."

As she dried herself she heard Corinne softly answering the phone, and when she came back into the room the girl was sitting on the bed, lighting a cigarette.

"There's someone coming" she said. "I have to throw you out now." Susan nodded. Neither of them moved. Each time Corinne sucked on the cigarette it made a sharp rushing sound like a fragment of tape played backwards. She said to Susan, "What're you doing here?"

"I came with a man."

"So what's new?"

"No" said Susan. "What I'm trying to say is he just brought me here. He didn't pay me. I wanted to come."

"How old are you?" asked Corinne.

"Forty-two. Why?"

Corinne repeated the number 'forty-two' and nodded, at the same time stroking her cigarette pack with her thumb. Then she turned to Susan and said in a different voice, "Are you in love?"

Susan shrugged. Water from her hair made darker patches on her dark dress, across the shoulders. She said, "He's an American."

"Even if I was in love" said Corinne "I'd never come here. Never. Not of my own free will."

"You don't know anything about it" said Susan.

Corinne bit her lip.

"Will you follow him?"

"Will I what?"

"Will you follow him" said Corinne "back to America?"

Susan laughed. "why should I do that?"

"Maybe you've got nothing else."

"Nothing else? What's that supposed to mean?"

"I'd follow him."

"You don't know him" said Susan.

The conversation appeared to be over until the girl - how old was she really? - seventeen? sixteen? - said:

"What did you do before this?"

"Before what?"

"Before the American."

"Do? I used to teach" said Susan. "I used to teach French in a school."

"Really? I'd love to speak French. Could you teach me? Well? Could you?"

Susan laughed. "How would I do that?"

"Each night we could make a time."

"But I'm not staying here" said Susan.

"I don't think you know whether you're staying or not" said the girl. "And besides, don't you think you owe me something?"

There's a knock at the door and immediately a man comes in. He's wearing a navy baseball hat with the letters 'NY' interlocked in gold. In his hands are the remains of a take-away in a styrene box.

"Oh-ho!" he says, wiping his fingers on the front of his ski-jacket. "There's two of them!"

Then he looks nervously from one woman to the other.

"So which is Corinne?"

"She is" says Corinne.

And after a brief pause they all three burst out laughing, the man the loudest, to show that he hadn't been fooled, not even for a moment.

* * * * * *

2) AMY

Each day she went back to the building off Bleeker, climbed the narrow staircase and tried Harding's door. She was well aware by now of the futility of this, but it was the futility itself that drove her on. The pale felt green door with grease marks round the lock was not Harding's, nor could it ever have been, but she returned to it, sometimes three or four times a day, checking the self-adhesive numerals against the number Harding himself had written on the scrap of paper, then ringing the bell, or gently knocking on the green paint, listening, listening for the slightest sound within, breathing, footsteps, driven, yes, by futility itself, which had become - or was this simply sleeplessness, despair? - both her motive and her goal.

She sat with her back against the door and must have slept because someone was tapping her on the shoulder. "Excuse me" said a voice. "Excuse me. I need to pass." Then, as Susan got to her feet, she added, as if explaining something to herself, "Are you looking for Harding?"

The girl's eyes were dark and unfathomable, and of such intense beauty that Susan had to first turn away from them before she could say "Is this where he lives?" The girl shrugged.

"I guess."

Then she licked her finger and began to rub at one of the greasemarks on the door.

"D'you know when he might be back?"

"Are you _British_?" said the girl.

"Yes" said Susan. "I've come from London to see him."

"_That's_ cool. I'd love to visit London. London - Paris - those are the cities I _dream_ about."

"D'you know when he might be back?" asked Susan.

"I didn't know he was _gone_" said the girl, rubbing harder and harder at the grease until it squeaked. "Would you like to come in for a while? I'm Amy by the way."

"Have you got a key?" said Susan.

"What? To his apartment? Why do you ask that? As a matter of fact I do have. But I meant to _my_ place. It's right on the next floor. It's kind of tiny, but that's Manhattan."

On the next floor was a door like Harding's, only canary yellow. As the girl put the key in the lock she lowered her voice and said, "Oh my boyfriend is in here by the way."

The boy was sitting on the bed, reading a book. He jumped up to shake Susan's hand, and introduced himself as Paul.

Amy's room was if anything smaller than the room in the Hotel Stuart had been. But it was much brighter, full of books, with museum posters tacked to the walls.

Paul and Amy sat side by side on the bed as Susan told her story, sometimes exchanging smiles, or touching each other's faces. They listened intensely, as if following a foreign language they only partly understood, clinging to the words they recognised. They seemed unable to see either the seriousness of her situation, or the irreversible nature of the events which had brought it about. For example, when she told them how all her money had been stolen on the train at Avenue X, Paul said, "Listen Susan, why don't you just wire your bank in Great Britain or fax them or go to Western Union or whatever? Even your _cards_ will most likely work in a machine over here. Money is a purely electronic commodity, you just need to make the right connexions." Susan tried to explain that she no

longer had an _account_, that she had withdrawn everything in London and lost everything here in New York, that she had _no money at all_, but she could see from their smiles that this concept was something they were unable - or unwilling - to grasp. So she began to modify her story, trying to leave out things - for example her pregnancy - which she felt lay outside their experience. But there was a limit to how much she could hold back, and when Amy asked how Harding fitted into all of this, she found herself telling them that she had given up everything for Harding, her job, her home, that there was quite literally nothing left, that she'd come to find him, that she'd followed him, and he was not there. That perhaps there was no longer any reason to find him, that perhaps there never had been ┌¹ at it was futile, but that she saw ɴo other choice, she was no longer capable of _thinking_ about anything else or even of considering what other things there _might be_ to think about, her mind was full of Harding yet at the same time it was blank, heavy, full of sand, bursting, she didn't know _what_ it was, or if she had a mind at all.

Paul and Amy said nothing as they watched Susan cry. Amy had tilted her head to one side and was gently moving it to bring the cut edge of her hair in contact with her upturned palm, as if judging the hair's weight. Very softly she said:

"I don't know, Susan. It doesn't seem to me such a big deal to've gotten into bed with Harding."

Susan lowered her head and wiped her eyes with the palms of her hands. Her face burned. She remembered what Amy had said on the stairs about having a key to Harding's apartment. She asked:

"Why? Do you sleep with him then?"

The question was charged with bitterness. She wanted to humiliate Amy in front of Paul, and perhaps punish them both for being so young and beautiful. But the two of them only burst out laughing, showing their white, regular teeth.

"That's her _father_ you're talking about" said Paul. "Mind you, with Harding, anything is possible."

"Don't be dis_gust_ing" said Amy, hitting Paul's arm. And the two of them began to fight, laughing and wrestling on the bed, until Paul succeeded in pinning Amy beneath him.

"He told me he didn't have any children" said Susan.

"Really?" Amy looked up into Paul's face and pushed the hair out of his eyes.

"I guess Harding would say anything to get laid - isn't that right?"

Amy pulled herself out from under him.

"That's a really sick thing to say, Paul. I think you should apologise to Susan. In fact I think you should fuck off. I think you should fuck off out of my room. What do _you_ know about my dad? What do _you_ know about what my father would or would not say to Susan? Go on. Get out. What kind of an asshole are you anyway?"

Before he left, he shook Susan's hand once more. He said he hoped there's been no misunderstanding, that he was very pleased to've met her, and was sure they would meet again soon.

******

During April 1993, in addition to **The Treatment** at the Royal Court, there are productions of Martin Crimp's **Play with Repeats** in Romania, **Getting Attention** in Hamburg and plans for a mini-series of readings of all his works in New York.

Martin Crimp

the treatment

by Martin Crimp

Cast in order of speaking

JEN	**Sheila Gish**
ANNE	**Jacqueline Defferary**
ANDREW	**Larry Pine**
NICKY	**Geraldine Somerville**
CLIFFORD	**Tom Watson**
SIMON	**Mark Strong**
TAXI DRIVER	**Marcus Heath**
JOHN	**Joseph Mydell**

All other parts played by members of the company

Director	**Lindsay Posner**
Designer	**Julian McGowan**
Lighting Designer	**Thomas Webster**
Composer	**Paddy Cunneen**
Sound	**Steve Hepworth**
Stage Manager	**Gemma Bodley**
DSM	**Alison Pottinger**
ASM	**Ruth Beal**
Student ASM	**Rachel Foy Smith**
Assistant Director	**Mary Peate**
Design Assistant	**Caroline Leask**
Costume Supervisors	**Jennifer Cook**
	Glenda Nash
Voice Coach	**Joan Washington**
Fight Director	**Terry King**
Choreographer	**Sue Lefton**
Illusion by	**Paul Kieve**
Set built by	**Terry Murphy**
Set painted by	**John Harkins**
Neon by	**Argon**
Sculptured figures by	**The Mik Weir Workshop**
Photographer	**John Haynes**
Leaflet Designs	**Sightlines**
	Loft

There will be one interval of fifteen minutes

The Royal Court would like to thank the following people: champagne bottles donated by Moet & Chandon; Budweiser donated by Anheuser Busch; lighters, cigarette cases and pens loaned by Colibri of London; sake bowls loaned by Benihana Restaurant, 100 Avenue Road, NW3 071 586 9508 & Asuka Restaurant, 209A Baker Street, NW1 071 486 5026; telephone by British Telecom Plc; desk lamp loaned by Artemide G/B Ltd, 17-19 Neal Street, WC2; Royal Court Hotel; Perrier UK Ltd; Japanes food supplied by Muji, 26 Great Marlborough Street, W1; Deryk & Davey at Rada; Alistair Galbraith.

Wardrobe care by Persil and Comfort; Cordless Drill by Makita Electric (UK) Ltd.; watches by The Timex Corporation; refrigerators by Electrolux and Philips Major Appliances Ltd.; kettles for rehearsals by Morphy Richards; video for casting purposes by Hitachi; backstage coffee machine by West 9; furniture by Knoll International; freezer for backstage use supplied by Zanussi Ltd 'Now that's a good idea.' Hair by Carole at Edmond's, 19 Beauchamp Place, SW3. Thanks to Casio for use of DAT equipment; closed circuit TV cameras and monitors by Mitsubishi UK Ltd. Natural spring water from Wye Spring Water, 149 Sloane Street, London SW1, tel. 071-730 6977. Overhead projector from W.H. Smith. The London Trophy Company, 653 Holloway Road, N19, 071 272 6245.

BIOGRAPHIES

MARTIN CRIMP

For the Royal Court: Getting Attention, No One Sees the Video

Other stage plays include: Play With Repeats (1989); Dealing With Clair (1988); Definitely the Bahamas (1987); Four Attempted Acts (1984); Living Remains (1982).

Radio plays include: Dealing With Clair (1991); Definitely the Bahamas (1986); Three Attempted Acts (1985).

Residencies and Awards: New Dramatists, New York (1991 exchange with Royal Court); Arts Council Theatre Writing Bursary (1990); Thames TV Writer-in-Residence (1988/9 Orange Tree Theatre); Radio Times Drama Award winner (1986); Giles Cooper Award winner (1985).

Fiction: Stage Kiss (1990 London Review of Books).

PADDY CUNNEEN

Composer and Musical Director for Cheek by Jowl. Regularly composes for Royal Shakespeare Company and Royal National Theatre as well as occasional commissions for Radio and Television.

JACQUELINE DEFFERARY

Trained at RADA (graduated 1992)

Theatre includes: What the Butler Saw (Salisbury Playhouse). TV includes: The Bill, Kissing the Gunner's Daughter.

SHEILA GISH

Recent theatre includes: Electra (Riverside Studios & Paris); What the Butler Saw (Hampstead Theatre & Wyndham's Theatre); Sara (Cheek by Jowl tour & Lilian Baylis); The Debutante Ball (Hampstead Theatre); When She Danced (Kings Head); Ashes (Bush Theatre); The Cocktail Party (Phoenix); Biography, Intermezzo (Greenwich Theatre); Rough Crossing (Royal National Theatre); A Streetcar Named Desire (Greenwich Theatre & Mermaid Theatre); A Patriot for Me (Chichester Festival Theatre); Uncle Vanya (Theatre Royal Haymarket); Berenice (Lyric Theatre, Hammersmith); Vieux Carre (Theatre Roayl, Nottingham & Piccadilly Theatre).

TV includes: Brighton Belles, Inspector Morse, Stanley and the Women, Resnick, Small World, Born in the Gardens, That Uncertain Feeling.

Films include: The Reckoning, A Day in the Death of Joe Egg, Highlander, Quartet.

Radio includes: Vieux Carre, Something Unspoken, The Secret Places of the Heart (all by Tennessee Williams).

MARCUS HEATH

Theatre includes: Trouble in Mind (Tricycle Theatre); The Merchant of Venice (Sherman Theatre, Cardiff & tour); The Boys Next Door, The Tinker (Comedy Theatre); Fences (Garrick Theatre); Comedy of Errors (English Shakespeare Co); Mr. Brown Comes Down the Hill (Westminster Theatre); I'm Not Rappaport (Apollo Theatre); The Man in the Glass Booth (St. Martin's Theatre); To Kill a Mockingbird (Mermaid Theatre); Sign of the Times (Savoy Theatre & tour); Measure for Measure (Royal National Theatre); The Big Knife (Albery Theatre); Night and Day (national tour); Clouds (Duke of York's Theatre); Connection (Living Theatre, New York).

Film and TV includes: Long Day Closes, Dempsey and Makepeace, South of the Border, Operation Thunderbolt, and many TV series.

JULIAN McGOWAN

For the Royal Court: Women Laughing, American Bagpipes, Blood, Downfall.

Other theatre design includes: The Changeling (RSC); Don Juan, Women Laughing (Royal Exchange, Manchester); Making History (Royal National Theatre); The Possibilities (Almeida Theatre); Heart Throb (Bush Theatre); Princess Ivona (ATC); Doctor of Honour (Cheek by Jowl); Prin (Lyric,

Hammersmith & West End);
Leonce and Lena (Crucible
Theatre, Sheffield); Imagine
Drowning (Hampstead); The
Rivals, Man and Superman,
Playboy of the Western World,
Hedda Gabler (Glasgow
Citizens Theatre).
Opera design includes: Cosi
fan tutte (New Israeli Opera);
Eugene Onegin (Scottish
Opera).

JOSEPH MYDELL

Theatre includes: Angels in
America (Royal National
Theatre); They Shoot Horses
Don't They, The Great White
Hope, Two Noble Kinsmen,
Flight, Worlds Apart, Macbeth
(RSC); As You Like It, The
Seagull, The Government
Inspector (Crucible Theatre,
Sheffield); The Boys Next Door
(Hampstead Theatre, Comedy
Theatre); The Life of Galileo,
Master Harold and the Boys
(Contact, Manchester); In the
Talking Dark (Royal Exchange,
Manchester); The Great White
Hope (Tricycle Theatre); The
Price of Experience (Traverse
Theatre, Edinburgh); Lyrics of
the Hearthside (one man
show/Royal National Theatre
& international tour; won
Edinburgh Fringe First Award);
Jelly Roll Soul (Edinburgh
Festival).
TV includes: Chancer, Tecx,
The March on Europe, Miss
Marple, The Care of Time,
Bergerac, Boon, Defrosting the
Fridge, A Shadow on the Sun,
Two Worlds, In Transit, The

Displaced Person, The Doctors,
Serpico, Bingo Long and The
Travelling All Stars.
Radio includes: The Slave
Trade.
Cabaret: Sunday Tea Dances
at the Ritz (regular
appearances).

LARRY PINE

For the Royal Court: Aunt Dan
and Lemon.
New York theatre includes:
Talk Radio (Public Theater);
Joe Egg (Longacre Theater);
End of the World (The Music
Box); Private Lives; Cyrano de
Bergerac (Vivian Beaumont
Theater); The Mandrake,
Gogol, Necessary Ends, The
Taming of the Shrew, Henry V,
All's Well That Ends Well (New
York Shakespeare Festival);
Alice in Wonderland, Endgame
(Manhattan Project).
Regional (U.S.) Theatre
includes: Night of the Iguana;
Hospitality; Morocco; Tartuffe;
A Thousand Clowns; Man and
Superman; The Doctor in Spite
of Himself; Much Ado About
Nothing; Comedy of Errors.
Film includes: Wall Street;
Plain Clothes; Anna; It
Happened at Night; Just Like
in the Movies.
TV includes: Hitman, Miami
Vice, Tales from the Darkside,
Gramps and the Globetrotters,
Kiss Me Petruchio, The Days
and Nights of Molly Dodd, One
Life to Live, As the World
Turns, Another World, Ryan's
Hope.

LINDSAY POSNER

For the Royal Court:
Colquhoun and MacBryde,
Death and the Maiden (& Duke
of York's Theatre & national
tour), American Bagpipes (&
Glasgow Mayfest), Ficky
Stingers, Built on Sand,
Ambulance, Downfall, Blood,
The Little Rabbi (part of May
Days), True Love Stories (part
of May Days), No One Sees the
Video, Sleeping Ugly (Young
Writers' Festival), Bucket of
Eels (rehearsed reading), 1953
(rehearsed reading).
Other theatre includes: The
Stillborn (devised); The Doctor
of Honour (Cheek by Jowl);
Leonce and Lena (Crucible
Theatre, Sheffield); Woyzeck
(Royal National Theatre
Studio).

GERALDINE SOMERVILLE

For the Royal Court: Three
Birds Alighting on a Field
(1992); A Jamaican Airman
Foresees His Death.
Other theatre includes: Romeo
and Juliet, Epsom Downs,
Yerma (Bristol Old Vic); Lady
Audley's Secret (Lyric Theatre,
Hammersmith); The Glass
Menagerie (Royal Exchange,
Manchester); More Than One
Antoinette (Young Vic).
TV includes: Poirot, Casualty,
The Black Velvet Gown, The
Bill, Business Affair.
Films include: Augustine.

MARK STRONG

Theatre includes: Pravda, Man of Mode, Animal Farm, Identity Unknown, The Idiot, The Importance of Being Earnest (Worcester); Macbeth, Translations (Contact Theatre, Manchester); The Plantagenets, The Man Who Came to Dinner (RSC/Barbican); Hess is Dead, The Futile Palace (RSC/Almeida); Richard III, King Lear, Napoli Millionaria, Fuente Ovejuna (Royal National Theatre).

TV includes: After Henry, Eastenders, The Bill, Inspector Morse, Tecx, The Buddha of Suburbia, T'is Pity She's a Whore.

Radio includes: Hobson's Choice, Double Cross, Ivanov. Film includes: The Story of Mary Liddell, Century.

TOM WATSON

For the Royal Court: The Catch, A Wholly Healthy Glasgow (also Royal Exchange and TV).

Other recent theatre includes: Walter (Edinburgh Festival & Dundee); At Our Table (Royal National Theatre); All My Sons (West Yorkshire Playhouse); The Ship (Glasgow & TV); Potestad (The Gate Theatre & Mayfest/award Best Actor, Gold Medal-New York International).

Recent TV: Prime Suspect, Govan Ghost Story, Your Cheatin' Heart, Making Out, Love and Reason (3 part series; soon to be seen).

Recent Films: Big Man, Silent Scream, From the Island (soon to be seen).

Radio: 35 years of broadcasting.

THOMAS WEBSTER

For the Royal Court: Other Worlds.

Other lighting designs include productions for ENO, Scottish Opera, WNO, Opera North, RSC, Almeida Theatre.

Most recent production: Queen of Spades (Glyndebourne).

THEATRE WITHOUT A PICTURE OF UTOPIA IS SCARCELY WORTH WORKING FOR.

A

Today's experimental theatre becomes tomorrow's mainstream and the boulevard theatre of the day after. The theatre riots of yesterday provide us with today's box office staples: Synge, Ibsen, Shaw, O'Casey. It was ever thus.

The route from the fringe to the mainstream is of great significance and Barclays New Stages helps to keep it clear. Perhaps it's of particular importance at this moment, when the theatre is redefining itself once more. The sheer exuberant theatricality of the best of the New Stages companies has much to teach those of us in the mainstream.

Artistic Director, Royal Court Theatre

BARCLAYS new stages

FESTIVAL OF INDEPENDENT THEATRE

ROYAL COURT THEATRE

Box Office
071-730 1745/
071-730 2554

Barclays New Stages is a unique six-year sponsorship programme for independent theatre. The scheme was devised by Barclays Bank to encourage and promote fringe theatre by providing sponsorship awards for original productions and support for an annual festival at the Royal Court Theatre. In its first three years, 1990 to 1992, Barclays New Stages sponsorship awards have enabled thirty new works to be created, performed and toured nationwide, and funded three festivals of independent theatre at the Royal Court.

The third Festival presents the work of seven talented companies

•On the BLUEBELL LINE, EAST SUSSEX•
LIMN GAZA: *The Joy of Return*
11-22 May 8.30pm. No performance on 16 May

•At the ROYAL COURT THEATRE•
EMILY WOOF: *Revolver* directed by Patrick Marber
1-5 June 7.30pm, Saturday matinee 3.30pm

PANTS PERFORMANCE ASSOCIATION: *Spam*
7-12 June 7.30pm, Saturday matinee 3.30pm

FORCED ENTERTAINMENT THEATRE CO-OPERATIVE: *Emanuelle Enchanted*
7-9 June 8.00pm

JIVING LINDY HOPPERS: *Echoes of Harlem*
10-12 June 8.00pm, Saturday matinee 4.00pm

LIFT '93 and Barclays New Stages present
GRAEME MILLER: *The Desire Paths* 14-19 June 8.00pm

MAN ACT: *Call Blue Jane* directed and written by Deborah Levy
14-19 June 7.30pm, Saturday matinee 3.30pm

For Barclays New Stages details: Kallaway Ltd 071 221 7883

THE OLIVIER BUILDING APPEAL

The Royal Court reached the ripe old age of 100 in September 1988. The theatre was showing its age somewhat, and the centenary was celebrated by the launch of the Olivier Appeal, for £800,000 to repair and improve the building.

Laurence Olivier's long association with the Court began as a schoolboy. He was given "a splendid seat in the Dress Circle" to see his first Shakespeare, **Henry IV Part 2** and was later to appear as Malcolm in **Macbeth** (in modern dress) in a Barry Jackson production, visiting from the Birmingham Repertory Theatre in 1928. His line of parts also included the Lord in the Prologue of **The Taming of the Shrew**. This early connection and his astonishing return in **The Entertainer,** which changed the direction of his career in 1957, made it natural that he should be the Appeal Patron. After his death, Joan Plowright CBE , the Lady Olivier, consented to take over as Patron.

We are now three-quarters of the way to our target. With the generous gifts of our many friends and donors, and an award from the Arts Council's Incentive Fund, we have enlarged and redecorated the bars and front of house areas, installed a new central heating boiler and new air conditioning equipment in both theatres, rewired many parts of the building, redecorated the dressing rooms and we are gradually upgrading the lighting and sound equipment.

With the help of the Theatre Restoration Fund, work has now started on building a rehearsal room and replacing the ancient roofs. The Foundation for Sport and the Arts have promised a grant which will enable us to restore the faded Victorian facade of the Theatre. So, much is being done, but much remains to do, to improve the technical facilities backstage which will open up new possibilities for our set designers.

Can you help? A tour of the theatre, including its more picturesque parts, can be arranged by ringing Becky Shaw on **071 730 5174**. If you would like to help with an event or a gift please ring Graham Cowley, General Manager, on the same number.

Laurence Olivier 1907-1989
Photo: Snowdon

'Secure the Theatre's future, and take it forward towards the new century. For the health of the whole theatrical life of Britain it is essential that this greatly all-providing theatre we love so much and wish so well continues to prosper.'
Laurence Olivier (1988)

THE ROYAL COURT THEATRE

Martin Crimp

Martin Crimp was born in 1956. His plays include *Definitely the Bahamas* (1987), *Dealing with Clair* (1988, starring Tom Courtenay), *Play with Repeats* (1989, written while Thames TV writer in residence at the Orange Tree Theatre, Richmond, where these three plays were first performed), *No One Sees the Video* (Royal Court Theatre Upstairs, 1990) and *Getting Attention* (West Yorkshire Playhouse, 1991). A short fiction, *Stage Kiss*, was published in 1991.

His work for radio includes the Giles Cooper Award winning *Three Attempted Acts* (1985) and the original version of *Definitely the Bahamas*, winner of the 1986 Radio Times Drama Award.

In 1991 he spent some time in New York as an exchange playwright with New Dramatists.

Note on the Text

An oblique stroke / indicates the point of interruption in overlapping dialogue.

Brackets ( ) indicate momentary changes of tone (usually a drop in projection).

A comma like this on a separate line

,

means a pause.

THE TREATMENT

A play in four acts
by Martin Crimp

Life as we know it has ended, and yet no one is able
to grasp what has taken its place . . . Slowly and
steadily, the city seems to be consuming itself.

Paul Auster
In The Country of Last Things

The genuine pain that keeps everything awake
is a tiny, infinite burn
on the innocent eyes of other systems.

.   .   .

Life is no dream. Watch out! Watch out! Watch out!

Lorca
Poet in New York

'It's really wonderful,' said Karl.
'Developments in this country are always rapid,' said
his uncle, breaking off the conversation.

Kafka
America

Characters

JENNIFER	40's
ANDREW	40's
ANNE	20's
SIMON	20's
CLIFFORD	60's
NICKY	20's
JOHN	40's
TAXI DRIVER	60's

also

WAITRESS
POLICE OFFICER
FEMALE MOVIE STAR
MAID
MAD WOMAN

JOHN, the POLICE OFFICER and the TAXI DRIVER are black ('African') Americans.

The play is organised so that the secondary parts can if necessary be taken by the actors playing NICKY and JOHN.

A CROWD is required in Act 4.1. If a real crowd is not feasible, it must be presented or implied by non-naturalistic means.

Time and Place

The place is NEW YORK CITY, the time the present.

ACT 1 – A day in June
ACT 2 – Evening of the same day
ACT 3 – A few days later
ACT 4 – A year later

ACT ONE

1 TriBeCa.* An office.

ANNE, JENNIFER *and* ANDREW. ANDREW *smokes*.

JEN. So he comes right over to you

ANNE. He comes right over to me.

JEN. He comes over to you. *I* see.

ANNE. And he sticks tape over my mouth.

JEN. OK. Why?

ANNE. To silence me. He wants to silence me.

JEN. To silence you.

ANNE. Yes.

JEN. Good. What kind of tape?

ANNE. Sticky tape. The kind of sticky tape you use for securing
cables.

JEN. Good.

ANNE. D'you know the kind / I mean?

JEN. We know the kind / you mean.

ANNE. The kind with a silver back. Sometimes silver,
sometimes it's black.

JEN. Silver is good. The glint of it. That's good.

ANNE. He always has this tape on account of his job.

JEN. Which is? (*To* ANDREW:) The way the silver would catch /
the light.

ANNE. OK. Yes. He's an electrical engineer.

---

*TriBeCa is the area of downtown New York forming a Triangle Below
Canal Street.

JEN. *That's* cool.

ANNE. So he always has this tape.

JEN. *That's* cool. Do you struggle?

ANNE. *Inwardly* I struggle.

JEN. Good.

ANNE. *Inwardly* I struggle. But he has a knife and calls me a bitch.

JEN. He calls you a bitch.

ANNE. Yes.

JEN. And there he is, with the knife, with the tape, this kind of tape with the silver back that's used for securing cables.

ANNE. Exactly.

,

Yes. / Exactly.

JEN. So what does he do? He cuts off a length of the tape?

ANNE. Cuts? No.

JEN. Uh-hu?

ANNE. That kind of tape / you can tear it

JEN. *I* understand.

ANNE. with your fingers. In fact I would say it is *designed* to be torn.

JEN. I understand. So he tears off a length (which is after all less awkward) / and sticks it.

ANNE. Exactly.

JEN. over your mouth.

ANNE. Yes.

JEN. To silence you.

ANNE. Yes.

JEN. This is in your home.

ANNE. Yes.

JEN. On Avenue X.

ANNE. Yes.

JEN *glances at* ANDREW.

JEN. And the knife?

ANNE. And the knife?

JEN. What does he do with the knife?

ANNE. The knife isn't visible.

JEN. Uh-hu. Not visible. OK.

ANNE. It's more the sense, the *sense* / of a knife.

JEN. The sense of a knife.

ANNE. Yes.

JEN. But this knife, the knife that is sensed, (she senses a knife), is this a part of his array?

ANNE. His array? What is that?

JEN. The array of items – tools – required by his job.

ANNE. You mean like the tape.

JEN. Exactly.

ANNE. I'm not sure.

JEN. OK.

ANNE. Because as I say I only sense it. And whether or not it's part of his array is beside the point because it's then that he begins to speak.

JEN. He speaks. He speaks to you.

ANNE. He speaks to me.

JEN. OK. (The knife worries me / a little.)

ANNE. He speaks to me. Yes.

JEN. How?

ANNE. How does he speak?

JEN. Tell me (yes) how he speaks.

ANNE. OK. Well, he's rapt.

JEN. Good. I see. No. Explain. What, this is rapt as in. . . ?

ANNE. Rapt as in rapture.

JEN. OK. Rapture.

ANNE. Rapt as in (I don't know . . .)

JEN. Rapture is fine.

ANNE. Or ecstasy I suppose.

JEN. We're happy with rapture. Unless you mean – d'you mean? – is what you mean that he is in some kind of trance. (The thought just / occurs to me.)

ANNE. A trance. Yes.

JEN. That's cool. He's speaking to her as if in a trance.

ANNE. More *from* a trance. As if *from* a trance. As if he's just. . ..

JEN. Waking?

ANNE. Waking, yes, from / a trance.

JEN. The silver tape. The glint from the light. The mirror image perhaps of his face – distorted – in the strip of tape. Tell me, has he been drinking?

ANNE. He doesn't drink.

JEN. Really?

ANNE. Not at these moments. *Later* he drinks. Later he goes out and drinks with his friends – Holly, Joel . . .

JEN. But now he begins to speak.

ANNE. Yes.

JEN. And what does he begin to speak about?

ANNE. He begins to speak about a parking-lot.

JEN. A parking-lot. OK. Does he? Which parking-lot is that?

ANNE. I don't know. It's outside a big store. At night. He talks about it at night. The white lines.

JEN. The white lines.

ANNE. The white lines that separate the cars.

JEN. OK.

ANNE. How they look at night when the cars aren't there.

JEN. Under the lights.

ANNE. Exactly. Those kind of orange lights they have at night.

JEN. Which now – OK, *I* see – *reveal* the previously concealed pattern of lines.

ANNE. Yes. And the low beds that divide the rows.

JEN. These are, what, these are beds of flowers?

ANNE. Flowerbeds. Yes. Which also have young trees in them.
He describes how they look at night.

JEN. How the young trees look at night under the orange
lights.

ANNE. Exactly.

JEN. Good.

ANNE. The appearance of the leaves.

,

JEN. And this is why he's silenced you.

ANNE. And there's a dog.

JEN. In the room?

ANNE. In the distance. It sounds distressed as if the dog's /
locked in.

JEN. So let me see if I've got this right. He's silenced you and
now – what? he's telling? is he telling? he's telling if I've got
this right he's telling the story of the women that he – here in
this parking lot – he has – what? – abused?

ANNE. I'm sorry.

JEN. Abused? Women I mean? Beneath the lights et cetera et
cetera – the young trees et cetera et cetera – the white lines.

ANNE. No. I'm sorry. He's abused no one.

JEN. Uh-hu? No one? Only called you a bitch. Only sealed your
mouth. Only threatened you with this knife which you as you
say you sense.

ANNE. He's abused no one. This isn't what he talks about.

JEN. OK. But you are – would it be fair to say you are
nevertheless terrified. Your eyes. (To ANDREW) Somehow I
imagine her eyes closed in terror.

ANNE: My eyes are *open* in terror.

JEN. Open in terror is good. Her eyes – yes – are open, wide
open staring.

ANNE. Absolute terror. Yes.

JEN. They're staring – of *course* they are – they're staring into his face.

ANNE. His hood.

JEN. What?

ANNE. Not face. He has a hood.

JEN. OK.

ANNE. A kind of leather hood.

JEN. OK. A leather hood. OK. Does he?

JEN and ANDREW *exchange a look.*

I see.

ANNE. And he continues to talk about the beauty of the world.
    That's his theme.

JEN. The world. Which world is that? What theme?

ANNE. This world.

JEN. You mean the world, this world we are / living in?

ANNE. This world we are / living in.

JEN. You don't mean some specific sub-world such as the insect
    world or let's say art – 'the world of Vermeer'

ANNE. No. This world. The world we inhabit. It's beauty.
    That's his theme.

'

JEN. OK so this man is weird.

ANNE. No, he's quite ordinary. I don't think of him / as weird.

JEN. Ordinary is better. It's better (you're right) than weird. He
    is weird – obviously – but he *seems* ordinary. (*To* ANDREW:)
    That can work.

ANNE. No he seems ordinary because he is ordinary. He is
    profoundly ordinary.

JEN. I might dispute that.

ANNE. That's what terrifies me.

JEN. His ordinariness. I see. I *think* I see. *Perhaps* I see. But
    what do *you* say?

ANNE. Say?

JEN. Yes. He talks a lot. This 'ordinary' guy. But what do *you* say? What's your *response*?

ANNE. I have tape over my mouth.

JEN. Of course. Sorry.

ANNE. I can't speak.

JEN. I'm sorry.

ANNE. How can I speak with tape over my mouth? Aren't you listening to me?

JEN. Naturally you can't talk of. Of *course* we're listening. So then – what? – he . . . strips you, touches you?

ANNE. I'm sorry.

JEN. The man, this man, he touches you?

ANNE. No.

JEN. *Inwardly* you struggle, but he overwhelms you, strips you, touches you.

ANNE. He just talks.

JEN. But as he talks he's touching your body, because the beauty of your body is part of the *world's* beauty. (*To* ANDREW:) We see her *body*, we see the / hood.

ANNE. He doesn't touch my body.

JEN. OK. Fine. (I see . . .) But he is . . . (I think I see now) he is forcing *you* to touch *him*.

ANNE. Not at all. No. There's no physical / contact.

JEN. He wants *his* body to be touched, admired.

ANNE. There's no physical contact.

JEN. But how can that be?

ANNE. It's just how it is.

JEN. No physical contact.

ANNE. Zero.

JEN. OK.

ANNE. Then he goes out.

JEN. With Holly, with Joel.

ANNE. With his friends. Yes.

JEN. Are you *sure* about that?

> ANNE *looks away. Silence.* JEN *glances at* ANDREW.
>
> OK why don't we break for lunch here. Andrew?

ANDREW. Japanese?

JEN. D'you like Japanese, Anne? Sushi?

ANNE. Sushi . . . that's . . .

ANDREW. It's fish, raw fish. Have you never had Sushi?

JEN. There's a place not far from here. Why don't we walk, get some / air.

ANDREW. Sushi is an art.

JEN. It's unpretentious. You'll like it.

ANDREW. We like it.

JEN. You'll like it. It's quiet. I should think you like quiet places, don't you Anne.

ANNE. I like clearings, clearings in a forest. Yes. I do. How did you know that?

ANDREW. It's not as quiet as a clearing.

ANNE. I understand that.

ANDREW. It's a restaurant.

ANNE. Of course.

JEN (*into intercom*). Nicky, have I had any messages?

NICKY'S VOICE. You're meeting Webb at two.

JEN. (*intercom*). Who the hell is Webb? We shan't be here / at two.

ANDREW. There's a certain amount of noise in a restaurant – there has to be.

ANNE: Orders. Conversation.

ANDREW: Exactly.

JEN (*intercom*). We're taking Anne to lunch right now. He'll just have / to wait.

ANDREW. What there is is a background, a constant background.

ANNE. It's like that in the forest too.

JEN. OK, let's go.

ANDREW. Shall we go?

He follows ANNE *out, talking to her.*

In the forest. Really? Is it?

2. Canal Street and Broadway. The sidewalk.

An elderly man, CLIFFORD, *is selling dishes and other household goods arranged on a blanket. A young man,* SIMON, *picks through the items. He's drinking from a bottle of beer inside a brown paper bag.*

CLIFFORD. I mapped out the course of my life very early on – in the fifties in fact. In the fifties I must've been your age, but already / I had decided

SIMON. How much is this?

CLIFFORD. (that one's ten) I had decided that I would divide each year of my life into two halves. In one half of the year I would do whatever was necessary to live – usually as it turned out in the summer months – meatpacking on 10th and 14th (of course I was stronger then) – or maybe / waiting tables

SIMON. And this?

CLIFFORD. (fifteen) last year for example I was security guard at the Museum of Modern Art because in recent years I've generally looked for something air-conditioned. And these modest jobs have given / me the means

SIMON. Fifteen for a *plate*?

CLIFFORD. to live because my outgoings are very low. That is Limoges. It belonged to my parents. It is not 'a plate', it is Limoges. And then the rest of the year, *each* year (the forks and spoons are solid silver) each and every year what I've done – generally through the winter months, the fall and winter months – is I've risen early, often in the dark, and I've sat at my desk, which is mahoghany and belonged to my

father and which I would never sell even though it fills my
room and I have to sleep curled up under it – I've sat at my
father's desk – he lost everything in 29 the year I was born –
I've sat at that desk and every year without fail I have
completed a play. That's forty-one shows in as many years.
Now there's a word for that. The word my young friend is
discipline.

SIMON. Discipline. Uh-hu. Is it?

CLIFFORD. As a young man I had a couple of big hits in the
fifties.

SIMON *smiles. He's not listening. He examines the silver.*

You don't believe me? In the fifties a couple of my shows
were playing on Broadway. I have the programs right here.
(*He pulls out some tattered programs:*) You see – big stars – *my*
name. And when I say Broadway I mean uptown – proper
theaters – not these holes that call themselves theaters where
people who call themselves actors mouth the obscenities of
people who call themselves writers. (*He chuckles.*) Two shows
on Broadway. Then after that, nothing.

He folds up the programs and puts them away.

SIMON. I like this fork.

CLIFFORD. Does that seem just to you? Is that justice?

SIMON. How much for the fork?

CLIFFORD. To dedicate your life to something, to an *art*.

SIMON. How much is the fork?

CLIFFORD. I'll take five for the fork. I send out scripts. Once
in awhile I have a meeting with a young person like yourself
who tells me my work is old-fashioned. I say to them that's
also true of William Shakespeare. (*He chuckles.*)

SIMON. Uh-hu? You say five?

CLIFFORD. It's antique.

SIMON. I'll take it. (*He pays.*)

CLIFFORD. I can see you value things like this, beautiful things like this.

CLIFFORD *pockets the five. He looks at* SIMON.

It's unusual to find someone on the street who values these
things.

,

Perhaps you know someone who . . .
I mean could introduce me to someone who . . .
Because I have *meetings* / but I never–

SIMON. I have no interest in the theater.

,

CLIFFORD. I see.

SIMON. I have no interest in any form of art.

CLIFFORD. Which is your right. I see that.

SIMON. I will not pay good money to be told that the world is a
heap of shit.

CLIFFORD. Listen, I write comedies. I've no / intention of –

SIMON. I won't sit in the dark to be told that it is an unweeded
garden.

CLIFFORD. A garden.

SIMON. An unweeded (that's right) garden. Or that man is
man's – OK? – excrement. And these are men who have
supposedly *thought* would you believe about the world, men
who are respected, who have a place in *history* . . .

CLIFFORD. Our own excrement? Is that *Biblical*?

SIMON. But what I say to them *is*, is the world is not a heap of
shit, *you* my friend are the heap of shit . . .

Nearby a car alarm goes off.

. . . the world is not a heap of shit because the sickness is *in
here* . . .

CLIFFORD. In the brain. OK. Listen–

SIMON. Right here – yes – in the brains of those individuals. People who practice so-called *art*, who urinate on their responsibility to others in order to burrow down into themselves, to drag up stories *out* of themselves.

CLIFFORD. You mean it's a chemical? Have you *studied* this?

SIMON. It could be a chemical, it could be an *experience* they've had.

The alarm grows more piercing.

CLIFFORD. In the womb.

SIMON. Wherever.

CLIFFORD. (Because I believe that people *do have* experiences / in the womb.)

SIMON. Wherever. It could be chemical. It could be their environment. But all I would say to them is get off of my back. Get the fuck off of my back because I do not *need* that.

The alarm is piercing. ANNE, JENNIFER *and* ANDREW *are passing on their way to the restaurant.*
SIMON *catches sight of* ANNE.

Anne?
Anne! Stop!

ANNE *and her companions stop. She stares at* SIMON.

It's me. Simon.

JEN. Who *is* that?

ANNE. I've no idea.

No one speaks. The alarm sounds.

SIMON (*to* ANNE). Who are those people?

ANNE. I don't know you. I'm sorry.

SIMON. But it's Anne? You *are* Anne?

ANNE. I think you're mistaken.

ANDREW. Come along, Anne. We should go.

He tries to move her on.

JEN. This neighborhood's not safe. We should've gotten a cab.
(*To* ANNE:) I'm so *sorry*.

ANDREW. We should go, Anne.

They move on, but ANNE *continues to stare back at* SIMON.

SIMON. ANNE!

ANDREW. Just keep moving. Are you OK?

SIMON. ANNE!

They've gone. The alarm still sounds.

That was Anne. That was my wife. I'm sure that was my wife.
Only she's changed something – her hair – her clothes. What
has she *done* to herself? Who were those *people*?

Car alarm stops.

They called her Anne. Didn't you hear them call her Anne?

CLIFFORD. Who is Anne?

SIMON. Anne is my wife.

A POLICE OFFICER *appears.* SIMON *is too absorbed to notice,
but* CLIFFORD *immediately begins bundling his things up in the
blanket.*

SIMON. She is my wife. Where are they taking her?

OFFICER. There's a child in the trunk of that blue Plymouth.
Chinese, male, about 8 years old. He's been shot through the
back of the head. He has no face.
Has either of you seen a Chinese male about 8 years old?
Did either of you hear a shot?
Did either of you hear a car security alarm?

Silence.

The OFFICER *notices that the paper bag has fallen from the bottle which* SIMON *still holds. He picks up the bag and thrusts it in* SIMON's *face.*

What's this?

SIMON. It's a bag.

OFFICER. And what is this?

SIMON. It's a bottle, a bottle of beer.

OFFICER. SO PUT THE FUCKING BOTTLE IN THE BAG YOU FUCKHEAD.

YES YOU YOU ASSHOLE.

I'M TALKING TO YOU.

THE BOTTLE.

IN THE BAG.

3   A Japanese Restaurant

ANNE *sits with* ANDREW *at a table for 3.*

ANDREW. I'll tell you what excites us, Anne.
It's because you're of the here and now. You're in the moment and *of* the moment. You're *real*. Because what are people *doing* out there? Out there they are listening to Schubert on authentic pianos. They are singing Bach at A-four-fifteen. They are squeezing into costumes, Anne, and mouthing words from old books. They are journeying on highly-polished steam-trains, looking tearfully out of the windows at a landscape to which one day they will no doubt return – older, wiser, immaculately lit.

He smiles at ANNE, *pours her a drink.*

These are people, Anne, who are allergic to the time we are living in. They can't eat the food. They can't touch another's body. They can't breathe the air. Their lives must be spent behind a screen or they will have a respiratory *crisis*.

ANNE sips the wine.

These are people who've given up. They say 'We do not have words to describe this state of affairs, this state of the world.' They say 'Words fail us.' But words can't fail, Anne, only *we* can fail.

ANNE sips the wine. A WAITRESS enters with dishes. ANDREW lowers his voice.

I love you, Anne.

WAITRESS. K

ANDREW. K is mine.

WAITRESS. G?

ANDREW. G is for Jennifer. She's sitting here. [*The empty seat.*]

WAITRESS. F?

ANNE doesn't react.

F?

WAITRESS puts dish F in front of ANNE and goes.

ANNE. I'm sorry? You *love* me?

ANDREW. Yes, Anne. Yes, I do.

She laughs softly in embarrassment.

Please don't laugh.
What is the level of discourse here?
To 'make out'. To go down on a man's penis. To lick a woman's anus. That is the level of discourse here. But I'm talking about loving a person's soul as revealed through their eyes. You have the eyes of the city.

He runs his fingertips over her eyes and down her cheek.

Please don't mention this to my wife.

ANNE. I don't *know* your wife.

ANDREW. Jennifer. Jennifer is my wife.

ANNE. I didn't know that.

ANDREW. You're not eating.

ANNE.. I'm sorry?

ANDREW. You're not / eating.

ANNE. Is Jennifer your *wife*?

ANDREW. *Eat* something. Yes.

ANNE. How can you love me?

ANDREW. Look, dip this in the sauce. (*He demonstrates.*)

ANNE. How can you love me?

ANDREW. You're saying to yourself 'I've known this man for only two hours'.

ANNE. Exactly.

ANDREW. You're saying 'What has this got to do with my purpose in coming here?'

ANNE. Exactly.

ANDREW. You are beginning to doubt perhaps what that purpose is. That's a natural part of the process.

ANNE. What process?

A moment passes. ANDREW *dips food in the sauce and holds it up to her lips.*

What process?

ANDREW. Eat.

ANNE. I'm not a child.

ANDREW. But you should eat.

ANNE. I'm not a child!

She knocks the chopsticks out of his hand.

(*Quietly.*) I don't want to be loved. That's not why I came.

She takes a cigarette. ANDREW *lights it.*

ANDREW. You've come to us with your story.

ANNE. Exactly. *Yes.*

ANDREW. You've come to us with your story, but once you
come to us with your story, your story is also ours. Because no
one's story is theirs alone. I hope you realise that – Anne.

A moment passes. JENNIFER *appears and takes her place.*

JEN. Everybody happy?

She takes ANNE's *cigarette from her mouth and stubs it out.*

Anne, you shouldn't smoke. You will die. D'you want to die?

All three laugh. JENNIFER *looks at her dish.*

Is this what I ordered?

ANDREW. G. Yes.

JEN. I ordered G? *Really?* (*To* ANNE:) No. I'm serious. D'you
want to die?

ANNE. I had no idea you were Andrew's / wife.

JEN (*calls*). Excuse me. Waitress.

Really? Does that surprise you? How long have we been
married now?

ANDREW. Sixteen years.

JEN. Who was that man in the street, Anne?

WAITRESS *appears. No pause.*

ANNE. I'm sorry?

JEN (*to* ANDREW). Sixteen? *Is* it? (*To* ANNE:) That man in the
street. Who *was* that?

ANDREW (*looking at* ANNE). Of course she doesn't want to die.
What kind of a question / is that?

JEN. Was that the man you described? The engineer? Was that
him?

ANNE. I'd never seen him / before.

JEN. And yet he knew your name. He knew her name. He was calling / 'Anne'.

ANDREW. Anne is a common name.

JEN. So is Jennifer. Anne is in fact less common *than* Jennifer, yet did he call 'Jennifer'? – no he called 'Anne'.

ANDREW. He was drunk, Jen. He simply found Anne attractive and he called out (which is after all typical of a certain / kind of man.)

JEN. OK he found Anne attractive which she may well be but he still could've called 'Jennifer' – that's what I'm saying, Andrew. But in fact he called 'Anne' and Anne stopped -

ANDREW. Anne stopped because that is her name. Isn't that right, Anne?

ANNE. I just heard my name and stopped. / *Obv*iously

ANDREW. And had he called 'Jennifer' then Jen would've stopped and we would be saying to Jen, 'Hey Jen, how come you are acquainted with that *ass*hole?'

ANDREW *and* ANNE *both laugh but* JEN *continues over.*

JEN. This is not trivial, Andrew. Because the man called 'Anne' and Anne stopped and if this is the man of whom she was speaking then this disturbs me, this disturbs me because one I understood that on coming to us she had severed all links with this man because two what if this man wishes to exert a right a moral *right* over a story which after all is partly his and because three Anne from what you have said this is a dangerous a dangerous man (I mean the knife the tape the world the young trees *Je*sus.)

WAITRESS *coughs.*

(Yes, one moment.) So I'm asking you to confirm that that was not the man.

ANDREW. She says it's not the man.

JEN. Anne?

ANNE. No.

JEN. It wasn't.

ANNE. No. He was just a drunk.

JEN. OK.

ANNE. I'd never seen him before.

JEN. We won't pay you to lie to us, Anne.

ANNE. I would never *do* that.

JEN. Well then that's fine. (*To* WAITRESS:) Yes, *I'm* sorry, you've just been standing there. I feel so awful because you may not believe this but I used to waitress and people treat you like / total shit, they really do. I mean Andrew

ANDREW. You really should eat something.

ANNE. I'm not hungry.

JEN. remembers don't you Andy when I used to work in a place called *Corner Café* and the girls (I was a girl then) we all had to wear these aprons that said 'Meet me at the Corner.'

ANDREW. 'Meet me at the corner.' That was a real / humiliation.

JEN. It's totally humiliating but the terrible thing Anne is that we accept these roles. 'Waitress' 'Customer' 'Victim' 'Oppressor' Is this G?

WAITRESS. G. Yes.

JEN. Well I'm sorry, I wanted what he has, I wanted K.

WAITRESS. You want K.

JEN. If that's no trouble.

WAITRESS. No trouble at all. (*She goes*.)

JEN. And who was it said? because didn't somebody say that the ex-waitress is the shittiest customer and the ex-customer makes the most servile waitress (*laughs*) yes that is profound, Anne, because it's true I treat these people like the scum of the earth.

Silence.

ANNE. So this is Sushi.

ANDREW. This must be the moment she's always dreamed of.

ANNE. I'm not interested in dreams.

JEN. We need something on paper, Anne. Did Andrew tell you? What has Andrew told you?

ANNE. Dreams are just circular.

ANDREW. Circular? Are they? How?

ANNE. In New York people dream of London, in London they dream of Paris, but in Paris they're dreaming of New York.

JEN. We really do need something on paper, Anne. Did Andrew not say?

ANNE. (That's what I mean by circles.)

ANDREW. Uh-hu. That's interesting.

JEN. Anne?

ANNE. Listen, I'm not a *writer*.

JEN. Just something on paper. You don't have / to *write*.

ANDREW. We can *find* / a writer.

JEN. Just tell the *paper* / what you've told *us*.

ANNE. Perhaps I need some time to think about this.

JEN. Of course you do. Yes. Think. Just a page. That would be cool. Because we love your story. We want to be *part* / of it.

ANDREW. It's our story too.

JEN. Exactly.

ANNE. OK.

JEN. OK?

                           ,

ANNE (*softly*). He hated me even leaving the *house*. He'd bring the groceries back himself on the way home from work. He collected coupons. He was always so happy when he'd used coupons to buy an item. He used to say 'Well Anne, look how much we've saved on this 10 ounce pack of freshly squeezed juice.' He tied me to the chair with pieces of wire. (*Faint laugh.*)

JEN. Just a page, Anne.

ANNE (*getting up*). I'm going to the Park. I need space to think.

JEN. The Park is a good idea. Then come back to the office. *You* know where to find us.

As ANNE *moves away from the table* ANDREW *follows her. At the same time* WAITRESS *enters with K.*

Is this K? You know, I don't think I'm hungry. I think we're going to leave. Oh *God* you come to a restaurant that's so *typical* no one wants to *eat*. (*She laughs*)

ANDREW (*sotto voce*). I *want* you, Anne.

JEN. Could we just have the check, please.

4 Taxi!

ANNE. Taxi! Taxi!

  The TAXI DRIVER *appears.*

  Central Park West.

DRIVER. Where *is* that?

ANNE. Where is what?

DRIVER. Where do you want to go?

ANNE. Central Park. Central Park West.

DRIVER. D'you know the way?

ANNE. Right. OK. Are you an immigrant?

DRIVER. I've lived in this city all of my life.

ANNE. Uh-hu. My apologies.

DRIVER. I know this city like the lines on my mother's face.

ANNE. OK. Just take me in that case just take me to Central Park West.

DRIVER. I was born on a hundred twenty-ninth Street. I've lived in this city all of my life, I'm not an immigrant.

ANNE. I didn't mean to *offend* you.

DRIVER. Am I offended?

,

ANNE. OK. I'm sorry. Let's just drive.

DRIVER. Am I offended?

ANNE. Let's just drive.

DRIVER. I picked you up on West 10th – is that right?

ANNE. I guess.

DRIVER. So I take a left here into Hudson, I pass Abingdon
Square and I join 8th Avenue. D'you see? It's simplicity.

ANNE. OK.

DRIVER. Just tell me when we reach Abingdon.

ANNE. OK.

DRIVER. I'd appreciate that.

,

Are you meeting someone in the Park?

ANNE. I'm sorry?

DRIVER. Someone maybe that you love. Someone maybe
whose hand you will hold, under the trees.

ANNE. I'm not meeting anybody. In fact I want I *need* to be on
my own.

Blast of horn.

ANNE. OK so this is Abingdon. (Listen, you've just gone
through a red / light.)

DRIVER. Someone whose life maybe is dearer to you than your
own.

,

Are we on 8th?

ANNE. Yes. Just go straight uptown.

DRIVER. Are you sure we're / on 8th?

ANNE. I *know* we're on 8th. (God the *filth* of this city how do we
live like this look at that woman and her *child*. The garbage
they are *eating* it no no no I can't / look.)

DRIVER. Are you sure we're on 8th?

ANNE. This is 8th and 16th. Yes. Just drive.

DRIVER. And the light's green?

ANNE. You have a green light.

DRIVER. Can you tell me if we come to another red.

ANNE. OK.

DRIVER. I'd appreciate that.

ANNE. Well OK.

Can I ask you a question?

DRIVER. I'm sorry?

ANNE. Can I ask you a question?

DRIVER. What question is that?

ANNE. Do you have a visual problem? Is your sight impaired?
Are you blind?

DRIVER. I was *born* blind. Right up there on a hundred
twenty-ninth street. Today you would operate, but back then
/ nobody even knew

ANNE (*intense panic*). *Oh* fuck. *Oh* Jesus Christ.

DRIVER. it was a medical condition. Because I was born out of
wedlock and my mother was just a child they thought this
blindness was a judgement from *God*. / They thought

ANNE. Let me out.

DRIVER. it was a *moral* issue not a health issue. Today it would
take just a simple operation at birth but she was a poor
woman and / she had *sinned*.

ANNE . STOP THE CAB! LET ME OUT OF THIS CAB!

Silence.

The taxi has stopped. ANNE *recovers her breath. Very slowly the*
DRIVER *turns his face towards her.*

DRIVER. Is this where you want to get out?

'

Or drops. They just put drops in your eyes at birth.

Very slowly he turns back again.

You have to tell me the fare. That's the situation here. One of trust. Some nights I have dreams about those drops. I dream that I can see. I dream about light which I have never seen.

ANNE. Just drive on.

DRIVER. Don't you want to get out?

'

I thought you were *afraid*. I thought you wanted to / get *out*.

ANNE. Just drive on to the Park.

5 TriBeCa. The Office.

JENNIFER *faces downstage, her mouth closed.* ANDREW *sits facing upstage in a chair, his back alone visible.*

ANDREW. D'you feel confident in Anne?

I feel confident in Anne.

JEN *empties the contents of her mouth into an ashtray.*

What do you think?

JEN. About Anne?

ANDREW *stands, zips up his pants.*

D'you think this is safe?

ANDREW. I think it's safe for *me.* (*Faint laugh.*)

JEN (*intercom*). Nicky?

NICKY's VOICE: Hello?

JEN (*intercom*). Could I have a glass of water, please.

ANDREW. (Not that I would endorse safety as a way of / living.)

JEN. I find her humorless.

ANDREW. Anne? Humorless?

JEN. What did she say when you told her you loved her?

ANDREW. That she didn't want to be loved.

JEN. OK. But she believed you?

ANDREW. *Oh* yes.

JEN. You looked into her eyes.

ANDREW. Yes.

JEN. You said. 'I love you, Anne.'

ANDREW. Yes.

JEN. And she believed you.

ANDREW. Yes.

Both faint laugh. NICKY *enters with a glass of water and remains in the room.*

JEN. It could be useful.

ANDREW. I think it *will be* useful. For her to feel as she now does that there is a commitment to her emotionally – / *personally.*

JEN. But what do you really feel?

ANDREW. I'm sorry?

JEN. What do you really feel about Anne?

ANDREW. What do I really / *feel*?

JEN. You looked into her eyes.

ANDREW. Yes.

JEN. You said 'I love you, Anne'

ANDREW. Yes.

JEN. And she believed you.

ANDREW. Are you *jealous*?

JEN. Nicky, is there something in particular you want?

NICKY. Yes *I'm* sorry but you have Mr Webb waiting / to see you.

ANDREW. Are you *jealous*? Because these are only *words*, Jennifer.

JEN. Webb?

NICKY. He arrived just after one for his appointment at two. It's now four. I just thought I would – I mean he asked me / to mention –

JEN. You say 'only words' but is it possible to use words without to some degree participating in their meaning? Because I'm not sure / that it is.

ANDREW. Perfectly possible. (*To* NICKY:) Who is Webb?

NICKY. He's a writer, Mr Wallace. He's been sitting out there for three hours.

ANDREW. You'd better show him in.

NICKY. Shall I show him in?

ANDREW. I think you'd better had.

NICKY *goes*.

(Three hours, that's / criminal.)

JEN. No Andrew, I am not 'jealous'. I'm simply questioning your level of insight.

JENNIFER *drinks the water as* NICKY *shows* WEBB *in*.

NICKY. Mr Webb (*She goes*.)

CLIFFORD. I'd rather you called me Clifford.

ANDREW. Clifford. Hello. Andrew.

They shake hands.

JEN. Jennifer.

CLIFFORD. Pleased to meet you, Jennifer.

They shake hands. CLIFFORD *looks around*.

Can I bum a cigarette from you?

JEN. I'm sorry, / I don't smoke.

ANDREW. Absolutely. Here.

He gives CLIFFORD a cigarette and lights it

CLIFFORD. It's just I've been out there for a couple of (thank you) couple of hours and I got through my whole damn pack.

He inhales deeply. JENNIFER *and* ANDREW *look at him in silence. He feels ill-at-ease and loosens his cravat.*

June – it's so humid. In Washington Square people are just standing under the fountains, young men and women just standing there with their clothes stuck to their bodies.

He drags again on the cigarette.

There's a bench where I usually sit.

ANDREW. A bench.

CLIFFORD. In the shade.

ANDREW. Uh-hu.

CLIFFORD. Listen . . . it's very good of you both to give me so much of your time. It's appreciated. I mean I realise the script is . . .

ANDREW. Please. Sit down.

CLIFFORD (*sitting*). I realise the script is (thank you) probably . . .

ANDREW. What script *is* that, Howard?

CLIFFORD. I'm sorry? I assumed that's what this / was about.

ANDREW. Do we have one of Howard's scripts?

JEN. Is it a *format* or *treatment* or what is it exactly? / (I'm not sure.)

CLIFFORD. It's a drama.

JEN. I'm sorry?

CLIFFORD. It's a drama. / I write comedy.

JEN. Howard says it's a drama. I don't recall this material. D'you recall this material?

ANDREW. When did we receive it, Howard?

JEN. (That's if we *have* / received it.)

CLIFFORD. About a year ago now.

ANDREW. OK.

CLIFFORD. You see six months of the year I do whatever is necessary / to live and for the other six months -

ANDREW. About a year ago. So that will mean that Nicky will've read it.

JEN. Exactly. Nicky reads everything. She is *incredible*.

ANDREW. She will've written you see what she will've done is she will've written / a report.

JEN. (*intercom*). Nicky, d'you have a report on / Howard's script?

CLIFFORD. Nicky. That's the girl on reception.

ANDREW. She's incredibly bright. She majored in Dance and Corporate Finance. She's here as an / intern.

JEN (*intercom*). *OK* could you make a copy and bring it in to us then.
She remembers it clearly.
She'll bring us a Xerox.

CLIFFORD *has smoked his cigarette down to the butt. He goes to stub it out but hesitates on seeing the fluid in the ashtray. He drops the butt in.*

ANDREW. *Tell* us something about yourself, Howard.

CLIFFORD. My name is Clifford.

ANDREW. *I'm* sorry.

JEN. Clifford Webb.

CLIFFORD. You may know my name. A couple of my shows were big hits in the fifties. (Of course that's before you were even *born*.)

JEN. That's very gallant of you, Clifford.

ANDREW. And what have you been doing / *since* then?

JEN. Clifford is very / gallant.

CLIFFORD. And they were playing on Broadway – proper
theaters – not these little holes that *call* / themselves theaters –

ANDREW. And what have you been doing *since* then?

JEN. Clifford would probably like to know something about *us* –
isn't that so? What would you like to know about us?

ANDREW. What *do* you know about us?

CLIFFORD. I've heard . . . very good things.

JEN. (That's cool.)

ANDREW. OK well what we are is essentially we are *facilitators*
meaning we are here because we wish to make connexions we
think of ourselves don't we Jen as a kind of chip, we're a chip
and out there are many many inputs –

JEN. Like the city itself.

ANDREW. Like the city itself exactly a *grid* into which things
feed a grid yes or chip for which we the facilitators provide
the logic the power while you provide people like yourself
provide the input the signal –

JEN. So this could be an idea / or a skill –

ANDREW. It could be an idea or a skill or often something less
tangible

NICKY *enters quietly and remains at the back of the room.*

          simply noise simply an input of noise pure noise
something intangible yes and random which nevertheless
comes on line it comes on line and generates the crucial
transformation.

JEN. The output.

ANDREW. The output. Exactly. Which is (we hope) / art.

CLIFFORD. Noise.

ANDREW. The kind of background you find (noise, yes) in a
restaurant or a forest. Something which both is and is not
silence.

(*Turns to* NICKY.) Nicky. Yes. (*She comes forward.*)

JEN. Or it could be an image, Clifford. A woman's face, her

eyes wide open in terror. Over her mouth a strip of reflecting tape. In the tape the image of her assailant's face forms and *re*-forms like globs of mercury.

NICKY. I have the report, Mr Wallace.

ANDREW. Excellent. Read it to us.

CLIFFORD. *Read* it? Listen, don't you want to –

ANDREW. To what? To wait?

JEN. Are you afraid? Don't be / afraid.

ANDREW. You've already waited three hours plus a year prior to that. I think we should just move on this. Nicky?

NICKY *reads the report*.

NICKY. 'Clifford Webb.
The Tenant.
A drama.

ANDREW *offers* CLIFFORD *a cigarette and lights it*.

'A man in his sixties – Brooke – has spent a lifetime doing menial jobs in order to finance his secret life as a painter. He paints obsessively in a tenement building up in the hundreds, spending whatever he earns on paint and materials.

'He rarely goes out, but one night he ventures into an East Village bar where he gets into a conversation with a young couple. They are art dealers and amuse themselves by getting Brooke drunk. However they miscalculate, and after a few hours become drunk themselves.

'When the couple say they must leave, Brooke asks to come with them. The man, Ethan, objects to this but is over-ruled by Clara, the girl.

'In their apartment on Christopher they continue to drink with Brooke until – it's not quite clear how this comes about does Brooke suggest it, or does he merely amplify a hint of Clara's? – it is agreed that Brooke will watch Ethan and Clara make love.

'This he does from a wicker chair at the foot of their bed.

'Tacitly – that is with no spoken agreement – this arrangement continues night after night until Brooke becomes part of the household.

'He abandons his casual work and begins instead to cook and clean for the couple, as well as caring for their baby son. In return he is allowed to be spectator of their most intimate moments.

'One afternoon, driving across town, Brooke is killed in a collision with a fire-truck.

'From this point on we witness the progressive degeneration of the young couple's relationship. Without the gaze of Brooke they no longer have any desire for each other. And in the absence of desire it soon becomes clear they have no other bond. Ethan immerses himself in his work at the gallery for longer and longer periods until Clara, disillusioned with a world which seems preoccupied only with fragments and surfaces, finally takes their son and joins the Amish.

'Several months later the new tenant of Brooke's apartment discovers a concealed doorway. She calls in a locksmith. The door leads to a basement beneath the stoop of the tenement. Inside are a number of paintings.

'These are the paintings made by Brooke during his last weeks of his life. They depict Clara and Ethan and are a unique record of the beauty of the human form at its most vulnerable. They are the work of a master at the height of his powers.

'The new tenant however considers the pictures obscene. With a pocket knife she cuts the canvases from the stretchers and burns them.'

Silence.

ANDREW (*softly*). It's a mindfuck, Clifford.

JEN. This is a total mindfuck. Why haven't we seen this, Nicky?

   (*To* ANDREW:) Have *you* seen this?

ANDREW. *I've* never seen this.

JEN. Nicky?

,

ANDREW (*shakes* CLIFFORD's *hand*). Congratulations.

CLIFFORD. Thank you.

JEN (*to* NICKY). Well?

NICKY. I *tried* to show you this.

JEN. I don't recall.

[*simultaneous conversations*]

NICKY. I tried to show you this but you said not to waste my time with un-solicited / material.

JEN. I don't *believe* that.

NICKY. You said why was I reading it. It should be *shredded*.

JEN. Shredded? I never said 'shredded'. Are you trying to *embarrass* me?

NICKY. *I'm* sorry.

JEN. I never said 'shredded' Nicky. I have great respect for people's endeavors. *You* know that. It's a *privilege* to see people's work. If I said 'shredded' I was kidding you.

NICKY. OK.

JEN. OK?

,

ANDREW. You told us you wrote *comedies*.

CLIFFORD. There *are* some funny lines.

ANDREW. She *burns* the paintings. That is a *mind*fuck. You are a dark horse, Clifford.

CLIFFORD. I've used a lot of personal experience. *Feelings*.

ANDREW. Of *course* you have.

CLIFFORD. There's a sense in which *I* am *Brooke*.

ANDREW. It's a metaphor.

CLIFFORD. In a way.

ANDREW. And it's so *real*.

CLIFFORD. So d'you think this can be used?

ANDREW. Used? Of course it can be used. We would be *privileged* to use this.

CLIFFORD. For many years I've despaired. I'll be frank.

If something like this comes along I want it on my *desk*.

NICKY. It was *on* your desk. It was on your desk for two weeks.

JEN. I don't want to argue.

NICKY. Then I filed it.

JEN. I'm not arguing with you.

ANDREW. Don't despair.

CLIFFORD. This is the moment I've always dreamed of.

ANDREW. Of *course* it is.

CLIFFORD. Look at me. I'm *shaking*.

ANDREW. Have a cigarette.

CLIFFORD. Thank you.

ANDREW. Listen. I have an idea. There's someone you should meet. You should meet Anne.

CLIFFORD. Who isAnne?

ANDREW. Don't you think, Jen? He should meet Anne?

What?

(*To* NICKY.) You can go (NICKY *goes*.)

What?

ANDREW. I think Clifford should meet Anne.

JEN. Who is Anne?

ANDREW. *Our* Anne. Don't you think?

CLIFFORD. Who is Anne?

JEN. Anne. *Yes*.

Blackout.

ACT TWO

Evening of the same day.

1 Central Park.

> ANNE *lies on the grass with a blank sheet of paper.*
> *She pays no attention to two* MOVIE STARS *playing from Act V.2*
> *of 'Othello', their voices amplified by throat mics.*

MOVIE STAR 1 (*as Othello*). He, woman:
  I say thy husband; dost understand the word?
  My friend, thy husband – honest, honest Iago.

MOVIE STAR 2 (*as Emilia*). If he say so, may his pernicious soul
  Rot half a grain a day! He lies to th' heart.
  She was too fond of her most filthy bargain.

MOVIE STAR 1. Ha!

MOVIE STAR 2. Do thy worst:
  This deed of thine is no more worthy heaven
  Than thou wast worthy her.

MOVIE STAR 1. Peace, you were best.

MOVIE STAR 2. Thou hast not half that power to do me harm

  As I have to be hurt. O gull! O dolt!
  As ignorant as dirt! Thou hast done a deed –
  I care not for thy sword; I'll make thee known,
  Though I lost twenty lives. Help! help, ho! help!
  The Moor hath kill'd my mistress! Murder! Murder!

> *During the preceding speech* SIMON *enters, unseen by* ANNE. *The*
> MOVIE STARS *disappear. We become aware of the long evening*
> *shadows.*
> SIMON *watches* ANNE *for a long time before speaking.*

SIMON. (*softly*) Anne?

ANNE *is startled but turns to him slowly.*

You look different.
Have you changed your hair?
What have you changed?

ANNE. Nothing.

SIMON *takes her sheet of paper and holds it up.*

SIMON. What's this?

ANNE. What does it look like?

ANNE *tries to recover the paper but he lifts it out of her reach and folds it as he speaks.*

SIMON. I think it is your letter of reconciliation. I think you're trying to find words to express your sorrow and shame.

ANNE. I have nothing to be ashamed of.

SIMON. Everyone misses you.

ANNE. Who is everyone?

SIMON. They ask after you.

ANNE. I don't know them.

SIMON. They're *concerned* for you.

ANNE. I don't know them, Simon.

SIMON. Your hair used to be brown. Your eyes were blue.

ANNE. My eyes *are* blue.

SIMON. But not the blue they used to be, Anne.

He's made a paper flower. He gives it to her.

How are you living? You can't shop. You can't cook.

ANNE. They gave me an advance. They checked me into a hotel. I don't *need* to cook, Simon.

SIMON. Which hotel?

I hate Shakespeare in the Park. It pollutes the Park.

ANNE (*without interest*). Does it?

SIMON. Didn't you see it?

ANNE. When I snap my fingers you're going to disappear.

SIMON. I don't think so.

ANNE. You're going to disappear, Simon.

She snaps her fingers and begins to turn away. However he grasps her wrist.

SIMON. What do they want from you?

ANNE. Nothing. Ideas. Let go of me.

SIMON. What ideas? What ideas do you have?

ANNE. They want us to tell my story. It's nothing.

SIMON. You don't have a story. What story?

He's hurting her.

What story?

ANNE. Nothing. Simon. Just –

SIMON. What?

ANNE. Whatever I can recall. Childhood. That kind of shit like being swung up into the air by your father and screaming and screaming or being knocked down by the ocean for the first time when the salt water gets somewhere behind your mouth your nose you don't know where the water is you think you're going to die LET GO OF ME!

SIMON. Childhood?

He releases her. ANNE rubs her wrist and begins to laugh.

ANNE. You know what they tried to make me eat today. Raw fish.

SIMON. Raw fish. That's degrading.

They both laugh.

(*Gently.*) Come back with me.

ANNE. It's Japanese.

SIMON. Come back, Anne. They'll corrupt you.

ANNE. He tried to feed me with it. (*She laughs.*)

SIMON. 'He'?

ANNE. Yes.

SIMON. Who is 'he'? Is he the man?

ANNE. Of course 'he' is the man. What else / could he be?

SIMON. You looked right through me in the street. I felt
    transparent.

ANNE. Did I?

SIMON. He tried to feed you. Where?

ANNE. In my mouth.

SIMON. Obviously in your mouth.

Obviously in your mouth, Anne.

ANNE. *He* mentioned my eyes.

*She turns away and unfolds the flower, smoothing out the paper,
smiling to herself.*

I'm not coming back, Simon. I'm never coming back. I have
my own room. Money. People who are (because they *are*)
interested in me.

SIMON. Interested in corrupting you . . .

ANNE. Well perhaps I want to be corrupted. Perhaps I *need* to
be corrupted. I've spent my life with you behind a *steel door*.

SIMON. . . . people who feed you in the mouth, who give you
money to tell them what happened to you as a *child* –

ANNE. Not just as a child, Simon. They want to hear about us.
They want to hear about you. (*Faint laugh.*)

The distant sound of applause and cries of 'Bravo!' from 'Othello'.

Touch me and I'll scream.

She stands her ground smiling faintly at SIMON.
The applause and cries grow louder, carried on the wind.

2 The Japanese Restaurant

JENNIFER *and* CLIFFORD *eat with the movie star who played*
Othello. His name is JOHN. *The* WAITRESS *attends them.* JOHN's
manner is notably measured and relaxed.

JOHN. Damaged in what way?

JEN. I would say socially, wouldn't you, Clifford.

JOHN. Because I am wary of the equation 'black equals
    damaged'. I'm sure you understand that. I am wary of the
    equation 'black equals street'.

JEN. Exactly but this is not a street guy. This man is educated.
    He's a – what is he, Clifford?

CLIFFORD. An engineer.

JEN. He's an electrical engineer.

JOHN. Uh– hu.

JEN. And what distinguishes him – as I was trying to explain –
    is that he has a vision.

JOHN. OK. That's good. Vision is good.

JEN. So when we say 'damaged', John, we're talking essentially
    we're talking about a man who is *outside* of the society in
    which he finds himself–

CLIFFORD. Marginalised.

JEN. And when we saw your Othello (marginalised, exactly)
    your Othello tonight in the Park . . .

CLIFFORD (*to* WAITRESS). A little more Champagne, please.

JEN. . . . it blew my mind away . . .

JOHN. Thank you.

JEN. . . . it blew my mind away because – well because the

parallels are so striking, and I immediately knew you would
be so *right* for this.

CLIFFORD. I'd like to introduce a Shakespearean element.

He drinks greedily. The WAITRESS *goes.*

JOHN. You are the writer.

JEN. Clifford has only just come on board.

JOHN. I'm sorry, I don't know your work.

JEN. And what is exciting is that this is a true story over which
we have complete control.

JOHN *nods, reflects.*

JOHN. Jennifer and I go back a long time, Clifford, a long long
time. I remember her with hair down to her waist and bells
round her ankles, don't I Jen. (*Faint laugh.*) Look at her. She's
embarrassed. But why?

I can remember her lying down in the street to protest. I
remember because I lay beside her, Clifford. That's how far
back we go. Side by side. In the street.

We felt that our actions might transform the world. We felt
that if our own relationships were free of the tensions of race,
sex, money, then the world itself would alter. In the way that
if you begin to grow plants in a stagnant pool, over time the
body of water will become clear.

He laughs at the naivety of this idea.

We saw this happening not for ourselves, but perhaps for our
children. Not that we had children, Clifford. Since as I'm sure
you realise, it's one thing to hang out with a black man, but
something else again to marry him, to have his children.

JENNIFER *looks away.* JOHN *is amused by her embarrassment,
but not bitter.*

JEN. (I'm sure Clifford doesn't want to hear about our wasted /

youth, John.)

JOHN. And if I didn't still possess such a strong picture of the girl who lay down beside me to protest about something I have entirely forgotten, then I would not – Clifford – contemplate getting involved even for one moment in the kind of degrading shit that has become her trademark.

A moment, before JOHN *begins to laugh.*

Come on, Jen. A joke.

JENNIFER *joins in the laughter a little uncertainly.* JOHN *lays his hand on the back of* CLIFFORD's *neck – a good-humored gesture which nevertheless disturbs* CLIFFORD.

A writer. A man of principle.

He continues to laugh as CLIFFORD *tries to move out of his grip. The* WAITRESS *reappears.*

WAITRESS. I have a call for a Mr Webb? Clifford Webb?
CLIFFORD. Excuse me.

CLIFFORD *disengages himself and goes with the* WAITRESS. JOHN *watches him go, laughing and shaking his head.*

JOHN. 'Shakespearean element.' He kills me.

Silence.

JEN. I resent your description of our work, John.
JOHN. How is Andrew?
JEN. What you said was not true.

JOHN *simply laughs and makes a gesture of mock surrender.*

JOHN. How is Andrew?

JEN. He's fine.

JOHN. I hear interesting things.

JEN. About Andrew?

JOHN. About both of you. Very interesting things.

JEN. You've always been unbearable when you moralise.

JOHN. Moralise?

Again he laughs and repeats 'surrender' gesture.

A man in a hood.
He's damaged.
He's black.
He ties women up with pieces of wire.
He forces them to touch him.
He abuses them.
But he has a vision.

JOHN *laughs and shakes his head, apparently in utter disbelief, before becoming serious:*

I would want veto of cast.
I would want writer– approval.
I would require producer– credit.
I would require complete control.
Think about it.

He begins to laugh again. CLIFFORD *reappears, smoking.*

You know something. Jennifer. You're still beautiful.
You haven't changed. Don't you find this woman beautiful,
Clifford.

JEN. Is something wrong?

CLIFFORD. I have to go.

JEN. Are you going?

Without sitting, CLIFFORD *drains his glass of Champagne.*

JOHN. There's a kind of beauty that survives. *I* don't possess it.

JEN. Are you alright?

CLIFFORD. I must go. I need to work.

JOHN. It's been a pleasure, Clifford.

> JOHN *shakes* CLIFFORD's *hand.* CLIFFORD *goes.*

'I must go.' 'I must work.'

> *He laughs.*

3 Upper West Side. ANDREW and JENNIFER's apartment.

A chair. An ambiguous sofa/bed.

A uniformed MAID *lights candles.*
ANNE *sits on the edge of the sofa examining a gun.*

ANNE. Who does this gun belong to?

> *The* MAID *says nothing.*

I hate weapons.

> *The* MAID *says nothing.*

I nearly *sat* on it. Shouldn't it be put away somewhere?

> ANDREW *enters, unseen by* ANNE.

I said: shouldn't this be *put* somewhere?

ANDREW. She doesn't speak English.

ANNE. I nearly *sat* on this. Is it yours? I hate weapons.

ANDREW (*taking the gun*). It's Jennifer's. I'm sorry.

ANNE. What does she want with a gun? (*Faint laugh.*)

ANDREW (*shrugs*). Sometimes she feels threatened, that's all.

> ANDREW *puts the gun away. He tells the* MAID *that she can go.*
> *She wishes them goodnight and withdraws.*

ANNE. Is that Italian?
ANDREW. Spanish.

Silence.

ANNE. I've brought the page.
ANDREW. What page is that? The *page*?
ANNE. The page. *This* page.

She passes him the page. He glances through it.

ANNE. Jennifer said she wanted it.
ANDREW. Uh– hu. 'Jennifer said.'

,

ANNE. Is that the kind of thing you mean?

ANDREW *looks up from the page and stares at her. He screws up the page and tosses it away.*

ANDREW. Why did you come here?
ANNE. To bring you the page. Jennifer said–
ANDREW. 'Jennifer said.' Is Jennifer *here*?
ANNE. I don't know.
ANDREW. She's not. She's not here. She's out of town.

Silence.

ANNE *gets up to retrieve the page.*

ANNE. I'm sorry. I'll just / go.

ANDREW. Please don't go.

He goes up to her. He takes the paper gently from her hand.

We don't need this, that's all.

,

Drink?

ANNE. I lied to you.

ANDREW. Oh?

ANNE. It *was* my husband. The man who called out to me. And again tonight in the Park.

ANDREW. In the Park. Really? Your husband.

ANNE. Yes.

ANDREW. Tonight? What did he say to you?

ANNE. He asked me to come back.

ANDREW. To your Avenue.

ANNE. To Avenue X, yes. (*Faint laugh.*) He said I'd be corrupted.

ANDREW. And what did you say to that? To what extent did he mean 'corrupted'? (*He hands her a drink.*)

,

ANNE. It's just that Jennifer said–

ANDREW. 'Jennifer said.'

He laughs and this time she joins in and relaxes. She sips the drink and looks round the room.

ANNE. If he could see me here he would / kill me.

ANDREW. Jennifer tends to over-react. She panics. Now I'm the opposite (if you can have an opposite of over / react.)

ANNE. You *under*-react.

ANDREW. Exactly.

They both laugh.

ANNE. You under-react because you have no feelings. You are
emotionally dead.

She laughs.

The eyes of the city. What did you mean?

She drinks. Silence.

It's so hot in my hotel room I take endless showers. There's
no bathroom *in* the room so I have to cross the corridor to
the shower. The curtain is rotting especially at the bottom
where it's permanently damp there's a kind of black mold
growing on the blue plastic and people've left scraps of soap
which I use to wash because I'm permanently scattered in this
heat and I forget my own. So I take a shower with the scraps
of soap then it's back to my room. I throw myself down on
the bed and just lie there drying off in the current of air from
the fan which I keep on maximum. For the first time in my
life, my whole life, I'm completely free and alone and I can't
bear it.

She drinks.

I've never traveled out of this *state* and yet I think I must be
somehow jetlagged because I can't sleep but I can't really
wake up – is that what it's like? I just go from the shower to
the bed and back to the shower again and my thoughts are in
a loop: how I replied to the ad never thinking anything
would happen – then there was the call and the limo arrived
– it was so *long* and white and cool inside and the driver never
met my eyes – then you listened to my story and we went to
the restaurant where I must've made such a fool of myself
knowing nothing about anything, what to *order*, how to use
chopsticks, nothing, what to *say* to you, and I reply to the ad and
the call comes, and the limo comes, and I tell my story, and
we go to the restaurant and I just lie there staring at the fan
which is like a person a disapproving person shaking its head
going 'no no no I don't believe this can be you Anne no no no
no no no no . . .'

As she chants 'no no no . . .' she moves her head slowly from side to side in imitation of the fan, her eyes shut. ANDREW *comes behind her and gently takes hold of her head, stilling it.*

ANDREW. We could change your hotel.

She opens her eyes. She moves away, sipping the drink.

ANNE. I've escaped from the man who silenced and humiliated me. So why does it feel like I'm betraying him?

ANDREW. We could change your hotel. You shouldn't be in that kind of hotel. Does *he* know where you're staying?

ANNE. All the scraps of soap. I must smell of so many different people. . .

ANDREW. Does *he* know where you're staying? Might he harm you?

ANNE. Simon?

ANDREW. Might he? You said if he found you here he would kill you.

ANNE. That's just a figure of speech.

ANDREW. OK. Good.

ANNE. Because he wouldn't kill me, obviously. What he would do is kill *you*. That would be the most likely thing. Because he *can be* violent (did I not say how violent he can be?)

ANDREW. Simon.

ANNE. He wants to protect me, yes. (*Faint laugh.*)

'

Did I not say? He'd love this room. The furniture. The light.

ANDREW. Are you saying he's killed?

ANNE. Well hasn't everyone in this city? (Either killed or *been* killed. . .)

She laughs. She's drinking too much.

I thought that was what excited you. The 'present'. The 'moment'.

ANDREW. You couldn't begin to imagine what excites me – Anne.

ANNE. Really?

For the first time ANNE is a little afraid.
Faint knocking.
Knocking a second time.
ANDREW turns to the door.

ANDREW. Yes? Hello?

Knocking again.

Excuse me.

ANDREW goes to the door and slips out leaving ANNE alone.
She swallows the remains of the drink and puts the glass down beside the crumpled page which she opens out.
She lies stomach– down on the ambiguous sofa and reads the page to herself, mumbling the words aloud in such a way that they are not intelligible. Occasionally she laughs softly at what she reads.
During this, ANDREW reappears at the door.
He watches ANNE, unseen by her, as she mumbles and laughs.
Eventually she senses his presence and falls silent without looking at him.

ANDREW. Corruption, Anne, has three stations. The first is the loss of innocence. The second is the desire to inflict that loss on others. The third is the need to instill in others that same desire.

ANNE (*turning to him*). Which station are we at?

ANDREW shuts the door.

He approaches ANNE who moves onto her back. She expects and is willing to have intercourse with him – but not at all prepared for the sudden brutality of it.
ANDREW penetrates her without any preliminaries.
He comes immediately, immediately lifts himself away and drops onto his back.

CLIFFORD appears in the room – not through the door, but from where he's been standing in the shadows. He drags on a cigarette.

ANDREW. You're a dark horse, Clifford.

ANNE (*sits up*). Who is that? Get him out. Was he *watching* us? (*She gets up.*)

ANDREW. I'd like you to meet Clifford.

. CLIFFORD. This may not be the moment.

ANDREW. Clifford is your writer.

ANNE. Was he *watching* us? Get him the fuck out of here.

CLIFFORD. This may not be the moment. I understand.

ANNE. Get out.

CLIFFORD. I understand.

,

No. Really. / I do.

ANNE. A *writer*?

CLIFFORD. A couple of shows of mine were big hits in the fifties. Of course that's before you / were even born.

ANNE (*to* ANDREW). I thought we were alone.

ANDREW. We are alone, Anne.

CLIFFORD. I'm very interested / in your story.

ANDREW. He's very interested in your story. He just wanted to try something, to *experience* something / that's all.

ANNE (*approaching* CLIFFORD). To try something.

CLIFFORD. Yes.

ANNE. And now you've – what? – you've tried it.

CLIFFORD. Yes.

ANNE. So how was it?

CLIFFORD. Listen I understand exactly what you must feel at this moment.

,

ANNE. So what do I feel? Tell me – I'm interested – what I feel.

,

ANDREW. Anne. . .

> ANNE *spits in* CLIFFORD's *face.*

ANNE. That's what I feel.

> ,

CLIFFORD. I respect that.

ANNE. That's what I *feel*.

ANDREW. Clifford's an old man and also a very good writer. You don't have to *spit* on him. Jesus.

ANNE. I hope you *die*. Clifford. I hope you *burn*.

> *For a moment* ANNE *stands paralysed by anger and humiliation. Then she walks out, pushing past* JENNIFER *who has just appeared in the doorway.*

JEN (*calls after her*). Anne? Anne?

> ,

CLIFFORD. Listen, if I've offended anyone. . .

JEN. You're an artist, Clifford. It's your job to give offense. (*Calls again.*) Anne?

> ,

JEN. Oh god oh god I feel I've missed something. Have I missed something? Because there is a charge in the air, like when you rub fur on a stick.

> ,

ANDREW. How was your meal?

JEN. We made progress. Only Clifford deserted us.

ANDREW. He had to work.

JEN. I know (*She smiles at* CLIFFORD.) We all have to work.

She sees ANNE's *page where it's fallen on the floor.*
She picks it up.

JEN. What's this?
ANDREW. Her story.

Blackout.

ACT THREE

A few days later.

1 TriBeCa. The office.

JENNIFER, ANDREW, JOHN, NICKY, CLIFFORD.
Boogie–woogie music.
JOHN *dances with* NICKY, JENNIFER *with* CLIFFORD.
ANDREW *sits watching them, without pleasure.*
At a solo break in the music it transpires that NICKY *(and* JOHN
ideally) is an extraordinary dancer.
JENNIFER *and* CLIFFORD *stand aside, clicking their fingers and
shouting approval as* NICKY *and* JOHN *do their stuff.*
ANDREW *takes no part in this.*
He is the first to notice that ANNE *has appeared in the doorway and is
watching the dance.*
He turns off the music.
The dance stops.

Silence.

ANNE's *appearance has changed. Her hair is fashionably cropped. She
wears a very plain very expensive dress. She takes off her dark glasses
revealing eyes darkened by sleeplessness. She looks unwell.* JOHN *is
first to speak.*

JOHN. This must be Anne.

JEN. You look different . . .

ANNE. I changed my hotel.

JEN. . . . . it suits you.

,

ANNE. Am I late?

JOHN. We were just dancing. D'you dance? Are you a dancer?

JEN. This is John.

ANNE. John. OK.

JOHN. Very pleased to meet you.

He shakes her hand. JENNIFER *continues the formalities.*

JEN. Nicky you know.

ANNE *and* NICKY *acknowledge each other.*

Clifford you've met.

CLIFFORD *nods and smiles.* ANNE *simply stares at him.*
It grows awkward.

Let's take five minutes everyone.

Three conversations A, B and C now occur simultaneously.
A finishes first, then B, and finally ANNE *and* ANDREW *in C.*

A

JEN: John, you wanted to speak with me. . .

JOHN: It's a small matter but I feel we should resolve it now.

JEN: Tell me what's on your mind. [*cue* NICKY *in B*]

JOHN: It's a question basically it's a question of personnel.

JENNIFER'S *attention is on* ANDREW *and* ANNE.

The creep has got to go.

JEN: What creep? You say 'creep' – the world is full of creeps, John.

JOHN: You know the creep I mean.

JENNIFER *follows* JOHN's *glance.*

JEN: Clifford?

JOHN: Uh-hu.

JEN: But Nicky likes his work. She says he is / a great craftsman.

JOHN: Nicky is an intellectual, Jen. The qualities she admires are precisely the ones we need to lose. I would find it impossible to work with him.

JEN: So Clifford is out.

'

Will *you* tell him?

JOHN: I'm happy to tell him. Is there a contract?

JEN: Are you kidding?

JOHN: Then the matter is resolved.

They fall silent as they watch ANDREW *and* ANNE.

B

NICKY *is left with* CLIFFORD. *A moment's unease between them before* NICKY *speaks – cue 'Tell me what's on your mind' in A.*

NICKY: You're so like my grandfather. Of course *he's* dead. [*cue* ANDREW *in C*] My grandmother moved to Sun City. She's considering Cryotherapy.

CLIFFORD: Cryotherapy.

NICKY: Yes it's a process whereby your body is preserved after death in liquid nitrogen at or close to absolute zero.

CLIFFORD: I like to think my *work* will outlive me.

'

NICKY: I write a little myself.

CLIFFORD: Really? That's interesting.

NICKY: Yes I've published one or two novels and I also write in a small way for the theater.

CLIFFORD: Uh-hu?

NICKY: I guess I've just been very lucky because some people struggle for years and of course I've never suffered in the way you must've done (except when my parents divorced, *that* was hard.)

CLIFFORD: (Did they?)

NICKY: (My Dad had an alcohol problem. Yes.)

They fall silent as they watch ANDREW *and* ANNE.

C

As JEN *begins to speak to* JOHN, ANDREW *takes* ANNE's *arm and leads her downstage.* ANDREW's *cue to speak is* NICKY's '*Of course he's dead' in B.*

ANDREW (*with quiet concern*). You look terrible, Anne. Has something happened?

ANNE: I'm not sleeping.

                                                            ,

ANDREW: Why didn't you return my calls?

ANNE: What calls?

ANDREW: I kept calling you. I've needed to speak to you.

He touches her cheek. She flinches.

I've wronged you.

ANNE: I hate that man.

ANDREW: What man, Anne? Your husband?

ANNE: That man. The writer.

ANDREW: It was a mistake. Please. Trust me.

ANNE: I can't sleep thinking about it.

ANDREW: Trust me, Anne.

ANNE: About him.

                                                            ,

ANDREW: I've wronged you. (*He takes her hand.*)

ANNE: How can I believe anything you say to me?

,

Have you really tried to call me?

ANDREW: Every day. I sent you *flowers*.

ANNE: Were those from you?

ANDREW: Wasn't there a card?

ANNE: I didn't look.

ANDREW: Didn't you look?

ANNE: The flowers were beautiful.

ANDREW: Didn't you look at the card? Of course they were from me.

,

ANNE (*faint laugh*). I've never seen so many *colors*.

ANDREW: Didn't you look at the card? I want us to start over, Anne. I want you to come away with me.

Silence. ANDREW *realises that the others have become aware of the intimacy of their conversation .*

I'll speak to you / later.

JEN (*claps hands*). OK can we begin everybody.
Andrew. Anne. Clifford. Nicky –   would you like to stay?
Anne? You have no objection to Nicky staying? I feel she should be involved.

ANNE *shakes her head: no objection.*
ANDREW *lights a cigarette for her.*
Slight adjustments to positioning.
All wait for ANNE *to speak.*

ANNE. Could I have a glass of water?

> ANDREW *goes out to get it.*
> *All wait again.*
> ANDREW *returns, gives water to* ANNE, *and sits beside her again.*

JEN. OK. We're in your apartment. It's 7pm. He's brought some stuff home and fixed you a meal. Let's say: spaghetti. (*Laughter from* JOHN, NICKY, CLIFFORD.) You've been chatting about this and that. And now he comes over to you. Is that right?

ANNE. That's right. He comes over to me.

JEN. He comes over to you and he sticks tape over your mouth.

ANNE. Yes.

JEN. Why?

ANNE. To silence me. He wants to silence me. We've been / through this.

JOHN. That's very strange. Why does he want to silence you, Anne?

ANNE. Uh. . .

JOHN. Is it the sound, the *sound* of your voice, the timbre maybe of your voice?

ANNE. I'm sorry?

JEN. Is it the voice, Anne, or what the voice is saying?

ANNE. I guess it's what I'm saying.

JOHN. What are you saying?

ANNE. He finds me critical.

JOHN. Of what? Of him? You're critical of him? Why?

NICKY. (Isn't that obvious?)

ANNE. Not of him.

JOHN. (Not necessarily.)

ANNE. Not of him. No. More generally critical I mean this is of the neighborhood. Because he was brought up there and to him it's home, he just doesn't see the violence or the dirt, he feels I / exaggerate.

JOHN. What d'you mean 'brought up there'?

ANNE. Well his grandfather managed freaks on Coney Island in its heyday and his mother and father still run a bar down there to this day –   'The Lucky Throw' –   you may / know it.

JOHN. Because I don't see him, Jen, as having this kind of background at all.

JEN. We'll come back to that / John.

ANNE. In fact on our first date he took me on the Cyclone – you know, the old roller–coaster down there –   afterwards he said 'I've never heard anyone scream so much' (which was strange you know because I had no recollection of screaming I must've been / so *out* of it.)

JOHN. I don't see him as having this kind of background. Freaks. Bar–tender. No way.

ANNE. What d'you mean?

,

What does he mean?

JEN. Tell us about the tape.

ANNE. No. What does he mean?

JEN. These are just possible changes, Anne.

ANNE. What 'changes'? (*To* ANDREW:) What does she mean?

JEN. John is attracting a great deal of money to this.

ANNE. I don't want anything changed.

JEN. A great deal of money, Anne. Your new hotel. Your / *clothes*.

JOHN. Perhaps 'changes' is too strong a word. It's more a question of where we place the emphasis.

ANNE (*warily*). OK.

JOHN. OK?

,

JEN. Tell John about the tape.

ANNE. I explained all this before.

JEN. John would like to hear.

ANNE. Well he always has this tape on account of his job. (He's an engineer. He installs telephones).

JOHN. Is that a skilled job?

ANNE. I'm sorry. I've no idea. I really don't see that / it matters.

JOHN. Is he educated? Did he study?

JEN. No, I think John's right to be concerned.

JOHN. Did he?

ANNE. I think he studied for a while. Then he became disillusioned. (I don't really know the / details.)

JOHN (*to* JEN). Disillusion is good. I can do something with that.

NICKY. Tell me something: do you struggle?

,

ANNE. I'm sorry?

JEN. (Disillusion. OK.)

NICKY. Do you struggle?

ANNE. *Inwardly* I struggle, but –

NICKY. But not physically. Why is that?

ANNE. What point would there be? He's much stronger than I am and at least this way I know I won't be hurt.

NICKY. Because I think there must be a struggle. Are we saying she just *sits* there and lets the guy do this. I find that unbelievable. And besides I object very strongly to the idea of woman as victim, woman as dead meat.

ANNE. I'm not a victim. Dead meat? What is she / *talking* about.

NICKY (*to* JOHN). I think that kind of passivity is / totally degrading

JOHN. I agree. It's / unacceptable.

ANNE. I'm not a victim. Fuck *you*.

NICKY. 'Not a victim'. *That's* cool. (Of course / she's a victim.)

JEN. Nicky, can you / ease up.

NICKY. *I* say she struggles. *I* say she resists. I say how can she *tolerate* this treatment from a man?

JOHN. So it becomes violent.

NICKY. Of *course* it becomes violent.

ANNE. She knows nothing about this. Can't somebody / explain –

NICKY. You see: (*Indicates* ANNE.) this is not my idea of Anne.

JOHN. Now that's *very* interesting.

ANNE. Listen to me, this is my story, I've *lived* this.

NICKY. This is not my idea of Anne: passive? humiliated? victim? –   She's 'lived' it. Haven't we also lived?

JEN. Nicky, you have no / right to –

JOHN. Please. Let her speak.

NICKY. You've 'lived' it. OK. But what does that mean? What if what you've lived is in fact banal? Must we accept that? No. We have a duty not to accept that, Anne, a duty to ourselves, a duty / to *you*.

JOHN. I think Brooke is the key to this.

NICKY. I think Brooke could well be –   yes –   / the key.

JOHN. Tell us something about Brooke.

ANNE. Who is Brooke?

CLIFFORD. Brooke is the old man who watches you both.

ANNE. Excuse me?

JEN (*to* JOHN). Brooke is Clifford's idea, John. / He's not –

JOHN (*to* ANNE). He interests me. What's his background?

CLIFFORD. He does menial work but has a secret life as an artist. / Every day he –

JOHN. I'd rather hear it from Anne, Clifford. Anne?

ANNE. What?

JOHN. Tell us about Brooke.

ANDREW. She doesn't *know* about Brooke.

JEN. Clifford wants to introduce a voyeuristic / element.

JOHN (*to* JEN). Why doesn't she know about Brooke?

ANDREW. Brooke isn't real. *Wait* / a minute.

JOHN. Isn't real? You mean she imagines him? I don't / buy that.

ANNE. I don't know who / Brooke *is*.

JOHN. I don't buy that. He has to be real. He has to be *there*, in the apartment. (*To* NICKY:) Isn't that right?
He's there?

NICKY. Absolutely. He's right there. He witnesses / their sexual acts.

JOHN. He witnesses – exactly, thankyou – their sexual / acts.

ANNE (*increasingly distressed*). What sexual acts? There are no sexual acts. There is no struggle. There is no other person. Just Simon and myself. I've told you this. He doesn't touch me, he talks to me. (*To* ANDREW:) Why are they changing / everything?

JOHN. Of course he talks, Anne. People talk. Which is why we require dialogue. But the talking is only the build. He has a vision – accepted – but that is only the build. (*To* JEN:) Incidentally I'm not happy with this 'secret life' idea.

CLIFFORD. I'm sorry but who exactly is writing this?

JEN. (We have to talk, / Clifford.)

JOHN. We must have a release, Anne.

ANNE. But he doesn't touch me . . . He's *never* touched me . . .

JOHN. A release.

ANNE. He's not interested in that aspect of marrige. . .

JOHN. Now in this case the release is a sexual act –

NICKY. Series would be better.

JOHN. Series would indeed be better of acts witnessed by a third person, Brooke. (*To* JEN:) I thought we'd discussed this.

ANNE. Not with me. NOT / WITH ME. (*She weeps.*)

JOHN. Because your life is interesting, Anne. . .

NICKY. Absolutely.

JOHN. Undoubtedly interesting – up to a point. We are here to help you get beyond that point.

ANNE *continues to weep from exhaustion and strain.*

A moment passes.

ANDREW (*softly but firmly*). She's saying he only talks.
JOHN. Are you *defending* her?

   ANNE *begins to moan.*

CLIFFORD. What is it you have to say to me?
JEN. This isn't the moment, Clifford.

   ANNE *continues to moan –   a thin monotone.*

   Let's give her some space everybody.
   Anne, would you like some space?

   She doesn't speak. She seems oblivious.

   Andrew, Clifford, Nicky – John – I'm sorry – would you
   mind very much leaving the room so Anne and I can have
   some space?

   They do so. As they go JOHN *puts his arm around* CLIFFORD.

JOHN. Jennifer has asked me to clarify the situation, Clifford.
CLIFFORD. Uh–hu? What situation is that?
JOHN. Exactly. It needs to be clarified . . . (*Faint laugh.*)

   They go out. ANDREW *is last to leave, glancing back as he goes.*

   ANNE *remains moaning.* JENNIFER *comes downstage to where
   she sits. She moves the glass of water out of the way, then strikes*
   ANNE's *face with such force that she falls to the floor.*

JEN. You offend *John.*
   You fuck *my* husband in *my* apartment.

   ANNE *huddles on the floor.*

ANNE (*incoherent*). I was lonely.

JEN. What?

,

   WHAT?

ANNE. I WAS LONELY

JEN. You were lonely. Couldn't you just talk?

,

I don't know what to do, Anne. You seem to have taken everything and given nothing.

ANNE *begins to whine unintelligibly.* JENNIFER *looks on.*

I can't hear what you're saying. (God, I wish I smoked.)

ANDREW *slips into the room.*

I can't hear what she's saying.

,

ANDREW. Why is she on the floor?

,

JEN (*shrugs*). Perhaps you can communicate with her.

JENNIFER *goes out.* ANDREW *remains at a distance from* ANNE *who has completely surrendered to her need to weep and keen. He lights a cigarette.*

ANDREW. I'm forty–four years old, Anne, but I sit at my desk and I write your name on pieces of paper. A–n–n–e. Anne. Then I strike it out in embarrassment. When I told you I loved you I thought 'OK this will be useful, I'll have some control', but now I find I meant what I said. The words, just the words, brought the emotion into being, and look at me – I have no control at all.

Is it because you're real? We don't often meet real people here. We ourselves have no memories or stories. No

enchantment, Anne. We are the disenchanted. We started out
real, but the real–ness has burned out of us.

ANNE *pays no attention. She remains huddled.* ANDREW *crouches
beside her and raises her head by the hair, forcing her eyes to meet his.*

Come away with me. Now.

ANNE (*with effort*). I don't . . . want . . . to be loved.

There's a commotion outside. ANDREW *roughly releases his grip.*
CLIFFORD *barges in, followed by* JOHN *who is trying to hold him
back.*

CLIFFORD. This nigger tells me I'm fired. What right does he
    have?

JOHN (*gripping him*). Ease up, my friend.

CLIFFORD. What right does this nigger have to fire me?

He shakes JOHN *off.*

JOHN. It's OK. He's upset. It's understandable.

ANDREW. Firstly he is not a 'nigger', his name is John.
    Secondly John, it's not understandable, it's unforgiveable.
    And lastly Clifford, if I remember correctly you were never
    hired. You were never *hired*, Clifford.

*The crashing sound of a subway train terminates the scene. The
sound crescendos alarmingly, finally fading as the train recedes and
lights come up to reveal:*

2 Avenue X. A subway station.

*The station is at ground level. A black metal wall obliterated by grafitti.
Untouched is a sign reading 'AVENUE X' in pure white letters on a
black ground.*

ANNE *has just gotten off the train. She's alone on the platform.*
SIMON *appears. They look at each other.*

SIMON. This has cost me a token.*

ANNE. Couldn't you've jumped it?

SIMON. There's a camera.

,

This has cost me a token and I'm not even going anywhere.
(*Faint laugh.*)

,

(*Expressionless –   as if reading from a piece of paper, but staring at her.*)

'I'm not coming back Simon I'm never coming back I have
my own room money people who are because they are
interested in me perhaps I want to be corrupted perhaps I
need to be corrupted I've spent my life with you behind a
steel door.'
But here you are. Have you been waiting long?

ANNE. I just got off the train. No.

SIMON. The F.

ANNE. It doesn't mean I've come back.

,

D'you like my dress?

SIMON. Why?

The blind TAXI DRIVER *appears and passes along the platform to
the exit using a stick. He pays no attention to* ANNE.

ANNE. Excuse me. Can I help you? Don't I know you?

Can I help? Excuse me.

He's gone.

SIMON. You know that guy?

---

* to pass through the turnstile

ANNE. He drives a cab. Yes.

,

SIMON. A cab?

ANNE. What d'you think? [*of the dress which she spins to exhibit*]

,

D'you think I'm a victim?

SIMON. What of?

ANNE (*shrugs*). You?

SIMON. This has cost me a token, Anne. I'm taking time off work. What do you *want*?

ANNE. I want you to hurt someone.

,

It's so hot I nearly stayed on the train. I thought I'd stay on to Coney Island, maybe ride the Cyclone, d'you remember how I / *screamed*?

SIMON. *What*?

,

ANNE. How I screamed.

,

SIMON. I fixed the shower.

ANNE. Did you? Was it the washer?

SIMON. I changed the washer.

ANNE. That's cool.

SIMON. It still drips.

ANNE. Uh–hu.

SIMON. But not so much.

ANNE. Simon?

She takes his head in her hands.

SIMON. Nice dress.

ANNE. Thank you.

SIMON. Hurt someone.

ANNE. Yes.

SIMON. I have a lot of work.

ANNE. Are they making you work too hard?

SIMON. I'm always digging up the sidewalk. It numbs my hands . . .

ANNE. Your poor hands. . . (*She takes his hands*.)

SIMON. . . . so I can't grip things.

,

　　I was doing the dishes and I dropped a glass in the sink.

ANNE. Did it smash?

SIMON: Of course it smashed.

ANNE: I'm sorry.

SIMON. Of course it smashed. A shard cut me. The sink was full of blood. I can't grip things, Anne.

ANNE. But it was wet. It slipped.

SIMON. I felt sick. I hate blood.

ANNE. I know you do.

SIMON. And it was the glass Adam gave us.

ANNE. Did Adam give us a glass?

SIMON. When we were married, yes.

ANNE. I don't recall that glass. Are you / *sure*.

SIMON. Well now it's smashed.

ANNE. Adam your father? *That* Adam?

SIMON. Yes, it was engraved.

,

　It had our initials on it.

ANNE. Adam your father gave us an engraved glass?

SIMON. (When we were married, yes.) I mean I possess a skill, but they have me laboring, Anne. They make me dig like an animal.

ANNE. Why's that?

SIMON. I don't know.

I don't know. *Ask* them.

ANNE. It was only a glass, Simon. I remember that glass. It was just a glass out of the bar.

SIMON. It was not 'only a glass'.

ANNE: The initials weren't even ours.

SIMON: It was not 'only a glass'.

ANNE. Everything breaks.

SIMON. I refuse to believe that.

ANNE. (Everything *we* ever had. Cups. The shower.)

SIMON. I fixed the shower.

ANNE. Well everything else.

SIMON. I fixed the shower, Anne, and I know you hate because you've always hated and despised my family.

ANNE. That's not what I said.

SIMON. You hate them because they're good. They're simple. They're not interested in the *unknown*. They don't want – no – to break – like you – to break away or to burrow like you – no – to burrow into themselves like you into the dirt inside of themselves because we all have – yes good fine – we all have that dirt, Anne. I've burrowed into the city and I know it goes because yes it goes down, the city goes down as far maybe farther than it goes *up*. Down down down it goes, which is why we must stay pure, Anne, and good. Why we must look *up*. Life is a gift transmitted from one family to another, not a waste–product to be sent for analysis. You do not check into a hotel to reveal to strangers what goes on behind a private door. You do not reveal to strangers what goes on between *us*.

ANNE. Nothing *has* gone on between us, Simon.

SIMON. What did you mean: 'hurt'?

ANNE. And besides I have a lover.

Someone who loves me.

SIMON. Is he the one?

I fixed the shower, Anne.

ANNE. I know you did.

They look at each other.

3 The Japanese Restaurant.

Faint music. Wine on the table. ANDREW *alone, brooding.*
WAITRESS *appears.*

WAITRESS. Are you ready to order?

Silence.

ANDREW. What sort of music is this?

WAITRESS. It's Japanese music.

ANDREW. It doesn't sound Japanese.

Can it be turned off?

WAITRESS. I'm sorry?

ANDREW. The Japanese music. Can it be / turned off?

WAITRESS. I don't know, sir.

,

I could *ask*.

ANDREW. (Leave it.)

WAITRESS. Most people like the Japanese music, but I could ask.

ANDREW. No. Leave it.

,

Is life very different in Japan?

WAITRESS. I'm from Brooklyn.

ANDREW. OK.

WAITRESS. Would you like to order now?

ANDREW. I'm waiting for my wife.

WAITRESS. Of course.

ANDREW. Why don't you sit down?

WAITRESS. I can't sit down.

ANDREW. But would you like to?

WAITRESS. Not really, no.

,

ANDREW (*taking out card*). Listen . . . it's quite possible that we could use you for something. We're always looking out for new material, ideas.

She looks at the card and puts it back on the table.

WAITRESS. I don't want to be used, thank you.

ANDREW. Uh–hu? I thought that's why people waited tables – to be discovered.

WAITRESS. I don't want to be discovered.

ANDREW. Well that is your right.

WAITRESS. OK?

ANDREW. OK.

They laugh quietly together.
JENNIFER *arrives.*

JENNIFER. I'm late. *I'm* sorry. Did you order for me?

ANDREW. I didn't know what you'd want.

JEN. (He didn't know what I'd want.) Don't I always have K?
I'll have K.

,

Andrew?

ANDREW. What? Yes. Sorry. The same.

WAITRESS *goes.* JENNIFER *pours herself wine and drinks,*
scrutinising ANDREW *who continues to brood.*

JEN. *Defending* her in front of John I was so *embarrassed.*

,

ANDREW. Would you call this music Japanese?

JEN. I've been talking to him for hours, Andrew. (What music?)
Literally for hours. *Calming* him. There *is* no music.

The music has indeed stopped.

Calming him, Andrew.

,

ANDREW. I'm going, Jennifer.

JEN. *I* see. Good. Yes. Go. I've never seen him so mad. He
threatened to withdraw everything, the finance, his *name.*

,

Well aren't you going?

He averts his eyes.

The truth is Andrew is that you will never go. Go where?
With whom? With Anne? Go with Anne is that the idea? who

is at most half your age and in all likelihood mentally
(judging by her behavior today) deficient and what? meet her
parents in the Lucky Throw?

ANDREW. (That's not her parents, that's / his.)

JEN. Have *babies*? Move into the *suburb*? Barbecue a pig on the
fourth of *July*? Put up your / *flag*?

ANDREW. That's not the only alternative.

JEN. Fine. Go.

ANDREW *makes no move*. WAITRESS *appears with dishes*.

WAITRESS. I got them to stop the music.

ANDREW. (Thank you.)

WAITRESS *goes*.

JEN. Are you *crying*?

He averts his eyes. JENNIFER *begins to eat*.

JEN. I worry about you, Andrew.

She continues to eat, choosing her moment.

John said something very interesting. He said 'What if there
is no such man?'

ANDREW *looks at her*.

Exactly. 'What if there is no such man?' What if Anne is lying?
Because John can't come to terms with what she says. He
doesn't find any truth there. The man she describes is too
weird, he is too weird Andrew to be plausible. And to 've
married him? To 've experienced those humiliations day after
day? Well Nicky was right. It's not believable. There is no
man. There is just Anne and her imagination. The hood? The
tape? The young trees?

She continues to eat.

She has invented those things in order to exploit us. You're not eating. Here.

She holds up some food for him to eat. He doesn't move. She eats it herself.

Incidentally, you may like to know she's gone. Yes. She checked out of the hotel. (I guess it was inevitable.)

ANDREW. Anne is lying?

JEN. They showed me her room. It's full of dead flowers. Your eyes are red. You look / terrible.

ANDREW. She's lying?

JEN. Had you never thought of that?

,

(Yes she checked out right after the meeting. Her account has been closed naturally. The fax / has gone out.)

ANDREW. Let's leave.

JEN. Leave.

ANDREW. Yes. Come with me. I have to get out.

JEN. Keep your voice down. What d'you mean, get out?

ANDREW. Get out. Now.

JEN. Out of the restaurant? Andrew?

ANDREW. I feel sick.

JEN. Are you sick? What is it?

ANDREW. I need some air. (I *believed* in her.)

JEN. You *have* some air. This room is full / of air.

ANDREW. I want to go. I want to leave.

JEN. Right now?

ANDREW. I want to leave the restaurant, yes.

,

JEN. There's no air out there, Andrew. Out there it's eighty degrees.

ANDREW. I want to *get out*, Jennifer.

WAITRESS (*coming over*). Is he alright?

JEN. He feels a little sick. I think we should have the check.

WAITRESS *goes*.

ANDREW. I need to be outside (*He stands*.)

JEN. I'll call a cab. D'you need the bathroom?

ANDREW. I want to walk.

JEN. *Can* you walk?

ANDREW. Of course I can walk.

JEN. Is this about Anne?

ANDREW. Yes it's about Anne. Of course it's about Anne.

JEN. Forget about her Andrew. She's gone. (Those flowers, they were completely dry, they / crumbled.)

ANDREW. I'm frightened.

JEN. We closed the account. Don't be frightened.

ANDREW. I believed in her.

JEN. We all believed in her.

ANDREW. I *loved* her.

JEN. So did we all love her. But it doesn't affect the work. The work's unaffected.

ANDREW. She lied to us? To me? Are you sure?

JEN. In fact the buzz in good. Already the buzz is good. John ended up being very / positive.

ANDREW. I need to be outside.

JEN (*looking for the* WAITRESS). Where is that girl? Did you have a jacket? Is this jacket yours?

ANDREW. I don't know.

JEN. It looks like yours.

ANDREW. Is it?

JEN (*helping him into the jacket*). You need me, Andrew. You need me to help you.

ANDREW. I know.

JEN. You're too easily deceived. You lack insight.

ANDREW. I know. I'm sorry. She's a bitch.

JEN. John opened my eyes. A bitch (that's right) in heat, Andy.

ANDREW. I feel humiliated.

JEN. You have been humiliated.

ANDREW. It's frightening here.

JEN. Where *is* everyone? Waitress?

ANDREW. She *sat* here. She sat at this table.

JEN. Waitress?

ANDREW. She spoke.

JEN. The account's closed, Andrew. It's over.

4. Canal Street and Broadway. The sidewalk.

CLIFFORD *is selling dishes as at the beginning of the play. A* MAD WOMAN *is picking through the items. In a corner, unseen by* CLIFFORD, ANNE *and* SIMON *are watching.*

WOMAN. My kid has diarrhoea. He's had diarrhoea for three days.

CLIFFORD. Uh–hu?

WOMAN. Isn't that something? Three days of diarrhoea?

CLIFFORD. Quite something.

WOMAN. D'you have anything for diarrhoea?

CLIFFORD. You need a drugstore. All I / have is –

WOMAN (*picks up a bottle*). What's in this bottle?

CLIFFORD. It's silver polish.

WOMAN. But what's *in* it.

CLIFFORD. Silver polish is in it.

WOMAN. But what's in the polish?

CLIFFORD. I'm sorry.

WOMAN. You think because I'm poor I'm ignorant? That I would poison my child? But what I'm saying is is there are things *in* things. You say 'this is polish' but inside the polish may be something good for diarrhoea just as in many *medicines* there is a poison. How come you have silver polish anyway?

CLIFFORD. It belonged to my mother.

WOMAN. Did she polish silver or was it polished for her?

CLIFFORD. The latter, I suppose. (That's very astute.)

WOMAN. 'The latter I suppose.' You have a very English way of speaking, you know that? Was your mother English?

CLIFFORD. She was from Europe.

WOMAN. And she brought all this silver? – and this china? – is that Limoges?

SIMON. Is that him?

ANNE. Yes. Go on.

CLIFFORD. It was a wedding present. Yes.

WOMAN. I'll take the polish. How much is it?

CLIFFORD. Fifty cents – but don't give it to a child.

WOMAN. D'you have children?

CLIFFORD. No.

WOMAN. Then you know nothing. What do you know? You could have children. You could have grandchildren. Then you might understand.

SIMON *comes over.*

CLIFFORD. My work has always come first.

WOMAN. What work is that?

SIMON. Excuse me.

WOMAN. Well I'm pleased to 've met you. (*She moves away.*)

SIMON. Excuse me.

CLIFFORD. Do we know each other?

The WOMAN *sits on the ground and begins to drink the polish.* SIMON *takes out the fork.*

SIMON. I have a complaint about this fork.

CLIFFORD. A complaint?

'

I remember. I sold you this for five. What's wrong with it?

SIMON. Look at these tines.

CLIFFORD. What tines? What is a tine?

SIMON. The prongs. Look at them.

CLIFFORD. The prongs are called tines? *That's* interesting. I didn't / know that.

SIMON. Didn't you know that? I thought words were your trade. Feel them. Yes.

CLIFFORD. They're like needles. They shouldn't be / like that.

SIMON. Exactly. I sharpened them on a stone.

'

CLIFFORD. Well you've done a very foolish thing. You've ruined a good fork.

SIMON. Don't call me a fool.

CLIFFORD. It was a good fork. It had a history.

SIMON. I have a complaint.

CLIFFORD. *You* did that to the fork, young man. I sold it you in good faith. Now I'm sorry / if you've –

SIMON. The complaint is not on my behalf. It's on behalf of my wife.

CLIFFORD. Now listen. I don't *know* your wife

SIMON. I think that you do.

CLIFFORD. Why did you do this to a good fork?

SIMON. I think that you do. I think that you defiled her honor.

CLIFFORD. You use some very strange words. Now listen –

SIMON. You looked at her. You spied on her. You defiled her.

CLIFFORD. I don't know your wife.

SIMON. I think that you do.

CLIFFORD *catches sight of* ANNE.

CLIFFORD. Listen . . . I'm sorry about the fork. Please choose another.

SIMON. I don't want another.

CLIFFORD. Look, take back your five. Take back ten.

SIMON. I don't want back my five.

CLIFFORD. So what do you want?

ANNE. DO IT.

SIMON (*matter of fact*). Revenge.

CLIFFORD. Listen, why don't we –

SIMON *stabs the fork into* CLIFFORD's *eye.*

ANNE. TWIST IT.

SIMON *twists the fork, lets it fall.*

The other eye. Simon!

As SIMON *backs away* ANNE *rushes forward and stabs the fork into* CLIFFORD's *other eye as he lies on the ground. Immediately a siren sounds.* SIMON *and* ANNE *run off. The* MAD WOMAN *starts to pick through* CLIFFORD's *things and drop them into a bag.*

JENNIFER *and* ANDREW *appear on their way from the restaurant to the office. They've not seen* SIMON *and* ANNE. *The* MAD WOMAN *picks up her bag and makes off, knocking against* JENNIFER.

JEN. Has something happened here?

WOMAN. His things. He asked me to take care of his things.

The WOMAN *slips away. The siren sounds.* JENNIFER *hangs back, but* ANDREW *approaches* CLIFFORD. *Neither recognises him.*

JEN. Has something happened here? Andrew? Don't touch him.

CLIFFORD. Help me,

JEN. Don't touch him, Andrew. You're sick.

CLIFFORD. Help me. I've been robbed.

JEN. My husband's sick. I'm sorry. He can't help. Andrew. Come *on*. This neighborhood's / not *safe*.

CLIFFORD (*turning to* JEN). I *know* you. I know your voice.

ANDREW. Clifford? Are you Clifford?

CLIFFORD. I *know* you. Who *are* you?

ANDREW. Who did this to you?

JEN. You're sick, Andrew. Come / *on*.

CLIFFORD. A man. It was a man.

ANDREW. A man did this to you? What man?

CLIFFORD. It was her husband.

JEN. This is not our problem, Andrew.

ANDREW. Whose husband?

JEN. This is not our *problem*.

ANDREW. Whose husband?

CLIFFORD. Who *are* you? I *know* you. Help me. It's dark.

JENNIFER *eases* ANDREW *away. They go.*

It's dark. Who did I offend?

Blackout.

ACT FOUR

A year later.

1 TriBeCa. The empty office.

In silence a group of formally dressed men and women file in until they fill most of the space. They don't speak. They wait.
Then, in this order, enter JENNIFER, NICKY *and lastly* JOHN, *also wearing formal clothes, jewelry. The crowd begins to applaud on seeing* JENNIFER, *the enthusiasm increasing with* NICKY, *at maximum on* JOHN.
The applause goes on and on as the three take up positions: JENNIFER *and* NICKY *at the back of the crowd,* JOHN *at the front, facing them.*
Finally JOHN, *smiling, gestures for silence.*
The mood is happy and relaxed. The crowd reacts to JOHN's *speech with unforced good humor and enthusiasm.*

JOHN. What is the meaning of success?
  The answer, my friends, is nothing.
  Nothing that is, unless it be success deserved, success merited.
  Tonight we have merited that success.

Applause.

Let me begin – a rhetorical device because I have of course already begun –

Laughter.

Let me begin with a word or two about Anne – the real Anne.

Stillness.

Art is nothing without life – and life is what Anne brought to us – *true* life – with all its fragility, inconsistency and banality – and yet at the same time – in Anne – both beauty and

strength. This is the room, the same room, in which she told
us her story and wept.

Stillness.

Our only regret is that she was not able to understand the
process of transformation by which life becomes art – a
process in which, at times, truth must be laid on a
Procrustean bed and cut here and there until it fits. (Not too
messily we hope.)

Laughter.

Talking of Anne brings me – a little too conveniently
I admit –

Laughter.

– but brings me nevertheless to Nicky. To Nicole. Nicole.

He extends his hand. To applause, NICKY *makes her way to the
front and takes* JOHN's *hand.*

When I first joined this project a year ago, Nicky here was
working on reception. She was answering *telephones*.

Laughter.

I'm quite serious. Wasn't that so?

NICKY. That's what I did.

JOHN. That's what she did. That is indeed what she did and
none of us at that time could've foreseen the stroke of genius
(my own as it happens) –

Laughter.

which would result in her – untrained – inexperienced as
she then was – in her being chosen to play Anne. But – as
you have all seen tonight – she does not 'play' Anne, she *is*
Anne. She inhabits Anne. At certain moments she is more
Anne than herself.

NICKY. (Thank you.)

JOHN. (It's true.) (*Gesture.*) Nicole.

More applause for NICKY.

Now I know you're all anxious to eat, to dance. Yes. I see it in your eyes. A certain restlessness.

Laughter.

But tonight would not be complete if I failed to mention the two facilitators of this project. Jennifer. And Andrew.

To applause JENNIFER *makes her way to the front.*

Andrew? Where are you?
We seem to 've lost Andrew.

Laughter.

JEN. (He's not well. He's lying down.)

JOHN. (He's lying down?)

Andrew is lying down. What've you been doing to him, Jen.

Laughter. JENNIFER *forces a smile.*
JOHN *takes her hand and waits for stillness.*

A year ago what was this project? It was nothing. It was a page.

JEN. (Less than a page.)

JOHN. It was less – exactly – than a page. But their tenacity, their violent need to create, transformed that page.

Stillness.

Jen and I go back a long way, a long long way.

JEN. (Not too far, John.)

Laughter. She forces a smile.

JOHN. Not too far – of course not too far –but far enough.
  Far enough to be part of a time when we seriously believed
  our actions would bring about – what Jen? revolution?
  peace? (fuck knows quite frankly)

Laughter.

  But that idealism –

JEN. (We weren't quite so vague, John.)

JOHN. (Not quite so vague but vague enough.) That idealism
  has stayed with us. It has stayed with us in our art. Now, it's
  fashionable to believe, my friends, that art changes nothing.
  But on the contrary, what I say to you is that art changes
  everything –

Tremendous applause.

  (*Over applause*.) It is the enduring reflection of our transient
  selves. It is what makes us *real*.

The applause continues until JOHN *gestures for silence.*

  And now, I believe – yes – my speech has ended.

Laughter.

  There is food. There is wine.

NICKY. (A band.)

JOHN. Even a band. Thank you all.
  (*He gestures to the door*.) Enjoy.

The crowd files out.

  NICKY *is first to move. She sits in a chair. She lowers her head.*

NICKY. Why do I feel so tense? John?

JOHN *comes behind her and begins to massage her shoulders, which
are naked.*
JENNIFER *doesn't move.*
The massage goes on in concentration and silence to JENNIFER's
increasing discomfort.
Finally, without stopping, JOHN *speaks.*

JOHN. How is Andrew?

,

Should you see him?

JEN. He may be asleep. He often sleeps.

JEN *lights a cigarette. Massage continues.*

JOHN. Jennifer is smoking. When did you start smoking /
Jennifer?
JEN. He just lies down and sleeps.
JOHN. Wake him.

,

Rouse him.

Faint laugh from NICKY.

Or is that no longer possible?

,

He's a weak man.
NICKY. He's not asleep.

,

JEN. I'm sorry?
NICKY. Andrew. He's not asleep.

JOHN. He's a weak man. Not only does he have many
weaknesses, but he gives in to them all. Perhaps that's his /
charm.

JEN. Have you been in to him?

JOHN. Because he does have charm – he can charm people away – *oh* yes.

JEN. Have you been into the room?

Massage continues.

NICKY. What room?

JEN. The room he was sleeping in. (Are you doing this / deliberately?)

JOHN. To think that when she married him I was crushed. Utterly. / (*Faint laugh.*)

NICKY. He was never asleep. He was not *in* the room. He's gone. (*To* JOHN:) Really? Were you?

JEN. Where?

NICKY. To Anne. He's gone to Anne.

JEN. How can he 've gone to Anne?

JOHN. ('Gone to Anne'. It doesn't surprise me. That's what I mean by / weakness.)

NICKY. He made me get out the old file. He wanted her address. That's where he's gone.

JEN. And you gave him the file? You let him go? You *said* nothing? When *was* this?

NICKY. I'm no longer your servant, Jennifer.

NICKY *and* JOHN *exchange a look and quiet laugh which confirm* JENNIFER's *exclusion.* JENNIFER *perceives this and leaves the room.*

(*Calls after her*:) The file's still out if you want it. It's green.

In silence the massage continues.

NICKY. Did you mean what you said?

JOHN. What did I say?

NICKY. Don't you recall? You made a speech, a great speech.

John?

She twists her head round to look up at him, but he stares ahead, continuing the massage.

JOHN. I recall nothing.

,

D'you hear that sound?

,

NICKY. I don't hear any sound.

JOHN. It's the elevator. It's Jen going down to the street. Down down down she goes. To the street.

,

NICKY. I don't hear it.

JOHN. Listen. (*He stills his hands.*)

Longest possible silence.

Blackout simultaneous with crashing sound of subway train which finally recedes as before to introduce:

2   Avenue X. ANNE and SIMON's apartment.

ANNE *is alone. She occupies exactly the same position as* NICKY *in the previous scene, sitting in a chair. However, unlike* NICKY, *she is tied to the chair and her mouth is taped shut. In the distance, intermittently, a dog barks.*
Close to ANNE's *face a battered fan slowly oscillates.*
She wears the same dress as in Act 3. It has grown ragged.

Banging at the door – which is offstage. The sound of the door opening. ANDREW *appears in the room, dressed in his formal clothes. He goes to* ANNE.
She makes no sound. He unties her. He carefully peels the tape from her mouth.

She wets her lips. No other reaction.

ANDREW. Anne?
ANNE. Who are you?

,

How did you get in here?
ANDREW. The door's not locked.
ANNE. That's a steel door. It's always locked.

,

Always.
ANDREW. It's Andrew.
ANNE. Andrew?

,

ANNE. You don't own that dog do you, Andrew? I worry about that dog. It sounds distressed.

ANDREW *starts to look around the room.*

You know *I'm* sorry but this is wrong. It's wrong to walk into someone's apartment like this. What are you looking for? We don't have anything. Do we look like we have things? Why are you dressed like that? Do I know you?
ANDREW. Is there somebody here?
ANNE. We've *been* robbed. A while back. There's nothing left to take.

ANDREW *picks up a piece of dark fabric.*

ANDREW. What is this?
ANNE. A hood. It belongs to my husband.

ANDREW *examines the hood. The dog is heard.*

I'm sorry but it has no value. Listen, if you own that dog why don't you feed it or exercise it or *care* for it / in some way?

ANDREW (*discards hood*). I thought you'd like to know it's a great success, Anne.

ANNE. What is?

ANDREW. Your life.

ANNE. I don't follow. A success?

ANDREW. Yes.

ANNE. Well. OK. Perhaps. I have enough to eat. I have my health. (*Faint laugh.*) Also I'm pregnant, so please – please don't hurt me.

ANDREW. You don't look pregnant.

ANNE. I even quit smoking. I used to smoke. I quit.

ANDREW (*hardly suppressing his anger*). Why don't you move?

ANNE. I beg your pardon?

ANDREW (*as before*). Why don't you *move*? Get out of that chair? I've untied you. That door isn't steel. It's not even *locked*.

ANNE (*calmly*). Move where? *I'm* sorry – this is my home. This is my chair. Why don't *you* move? Why don't you get the fuck out? (Dressed like that, poking about, Jesus Christ this is *my* / apartment.)

She looks away from him, rubbing her wrists.

ANDREW. I want you to come with me before he gets back.

ANNE. Before who gets back? What if I don't want / to come?

ANDREW. The man.

ANNE. What man? D'you mean my husband?

ANDREW. Do you have a husband?

ANNE. I'm pregnant. Of course I have a husband.

ANDREW. Simon.

ANNE. Yes.

ANDREW. Where is he? Where is Simon?

ANNE. Don't you believe me?

ANDREW. Where is Simon?

ANNE. Are you one of his friends? I never meet his friends. He prefers to go out alone. He tells me all about them, though.

ANDREW. Please, Anne . . .

ANNE. There's Joel – Joel's gay but he's very very funny –
and Max of course – and Holly who's just had a baby girl.
Then there's Ross who works for Adam behind the bar. *His*
cousin's a police officer. Which one are you? Are you Joel?

ANDREW. My name is Andrew.

ANNE. He's never mentioned you.

ANDREW. I'm not one of his / friends.

ANNE. I used to really crave to go out. My dream was to go
through that door. But now I see how wrong I was to crave
and how right he was to keep me in. Because last time we
went out together we did something really really terrible.
(*Lowers voice*.) You won't believe this, but we put out a man's
eyes. (*Faint laugh*.)

She continues to rub her wrists.

ANDREW. How d'you mean 'put them out'?

ANNE. Right out of his head. How else out?

She turns and looks straight at him. Her tone changes.

I know who you are.
I think you should leave.

SIMON *appears. He's drinking from a bottle of beer in a paper bag,
as when first seen.*
He looks briefly at ANDREW *and* ANNE.

SIMON. I need to take a shower.

ANNE. Is it hot out?

SIMON. It's still hot.

ANNE. What time is it?

SIMON. It's 2 am.

ANNE. You're back early.

This is the man owns the dog.

SIMON. What dog?

ANNE. The dog we always hear, Simon.

SIMON. (Pleased to meet you.) I never hear a dog, Anne.

ANNE. He never hears it. He imagines this neighbourhood is /
  peaceful.

SIMON. What sort of dog do you have?

ANDREW. I don't have a dog. I don't own a dog. I'm *sorry*.
  That's not why I'm here.

SIMON. Uh-hu?

,

In that case Anne is / mistaken.

ANNE. How was Joel?

SIMON. Joel wasn't there tonight. Why is he dressed like that?

ANDREW. My name is Andrew.

SIMON. In fact that's why we left. It's not so much fun without
  Joel. Andrew? *I* see. Is it?

ANDREW. I want Anne to come with me.

SIMON. Would 'Andrew' like a beer? What do you drink,
  Andrew?

ANDREW. I want her to leave. / Now.

SIMON. Anne, why don't you get Andrew a beer?

,

Perhaps you don't drink. That's very wise. My wife is
pregnant. She's given up – haven't you Anne? – tobacco *and*
alcohol. In fact the last time she drank / which was
approximately.

ANNE. (Please stop, Simon.)

SIMON. twelve months ago (stop? why?) the last time she drank
  she was raped by a complete stranger.

ANNE. I was not raped / Simon.

SIMON. Raped by a complete stranger, Andrew. This is in

we're talking a respectable apartment on the Upper West
Side where they have servants and candles and if they look
east they can see the Park.

,

Yes.

ANNE. (I was not raped.)

SIMON. So perhaps you don't drink. Do you drink?

,

Why don't you sit / down?

ANDREW. Anne, we have / to go.

SIMON. D'you see – Andrew – how the color's come back to
her hair – and to her eyes? (Go? I don't think so.) Look at
her eyes. They're blue again. Show him your eyes, Anne.
D'you see how the light comes from the inside? That's
because she eats properly now. No one's trying to feed her in
the mouth, Andrew. She eats good fresh things which I cook
for her. I shop for her, I cook for her, everything is done for
her, isn't it, Anne. Sometimes I *wash* her, I wash her body –
isn't that so?

ANNE. Sometimes he washes me. It's true.

SIMON. You see? Why don't you sit down?

ANNE. But I'll wash the baby sometimes, won't I Simon? That
is what you said?

SIMON. Of course you'll wash the baby.

ANNE. (*faint laugh*) I hate the way their heads flop back.

SIMON. You have to cradle their heads, Anne. I've told you.

ANNE. (Yes. OK. Cradle them.) It's kind of scarey. So many
things can go wrong. Pregnancy. Delivery. Infancy. Do you
have any children?

SIMON. Nothing will go wrong, Anne. Just cradle his head.

ANNE. I will take him out sometimes, won't I?

SIMON. Of course you'll take him out. He has to see the world.
The sky. Trees. The young trees.

ANNE. I'd like to go out.

SIMON. You can always go out.

Silence.

ANDREW. Can she go out now?

Silence.

SIMON. She can always go out, but she chooses not to.

ANDREW. Why don't you go out, Anne. Get some air.

ANNE (*confused*). What? Now? It's late. I . . .

SIMON. It's just that she chooses not to.

ANDREW. Yes. Go out now.

ANNE. I'm not really dressed. I . . .

SIMON. She doesn't *want* to go out. That's *her* choice.

ANNE. I'm not really dressed. My hair . . . (*she runs her hand through it*) look at it.

Perhaps for a few minutes, Simon. May I?

ANDREW. Go now.

SIMON. She chooses not to, that's all.

ANNE *hesitates, then moves very slowly away from* SIMON *and towards the way out. She breaks into a run and goes.*

This proves nothing.

Offstage, a single shot.
SIMON *goes out.*
A moment passes. ANDREW *doesn't move.*
JENNIFER *enters, holding the gun.*

JENNIFER. She *ran* at me. I just *reacted*. Why did she *run*? I *reacted* to that. It's so *threatening* here, Andrew.

Stillness.

She was running *towards* me. *At* me. There's no light, she *appeared. Don't* look at me like that. She appeared, it was a reaction.

Stillness.

I've been wandering this lousy project in a state of *total fear*, Andrew. Nothing is *numbered. Total fear. Why* did you do this? FUCK this. Are you now HAPPY?

She throws down the gun.
SIMON *enters. He looks at them.*

(*Softly.*) She ran at me. It was a threat. I reacted.

Long silence.

SIMON. My child.
JEN. Are you *Simon*?

Blackout and simultaneously CLIFFORD's *voice calling 'Taxi! Taxi!'*

3 Taxi!

Faint light reveals CLIFFORD *calling for a taxi. He's clutching a sheaf of papers. Throughout the scene pages fall from the sheaf and are swept away by a current of air.*

The TAXI DRIVER *appears as before.*

DRIVER. Where to?
CLIFFORD. Where is this?
DRIVER. 'Where is this'? Don't you know?
CLIFFORD. I *think* I know.

DRIVER. Well tell me what you think.

CLIFFORD. I think this is Canal Street and Broadway.

DRIVER. I think you're right. I think this is Canal Street. It feels like Canal Street.

CLIFFORD. Don't you know? Isn't there / a *sign*?

DRIVER. I've lived in this city all of my life.

CLIFFORD. Me too.

DRIVER. That's unusual.

CLIFFORD. Yes. D'you think?

DRIVER. Where can I take you?

CLIFFORD. Broadway and East 52nd.

DRIVER. There is no such thing.

CLIFFORD. But I was given the address.

DRIVER. Well I'm sorry but there is no such thing.

Sheets of paper continue to blow away.

What kind of place is it you want? I could take you to *West* 52nd and Broadway.

CLIFFORD. I have to deliver some work.

DRIVER. In the middle of the night.

CLIFFORD. Is this the middle of the night?

DRIVER. Certainly.

CLIFFORD. I didn't know that.

DRIVER. What kind of work is it?

CLIFFORD. A script.

DRIVER. Can't you mail it?

CLIFFORD (*gripping the paper*). Am I losing pages?

DRIVER. A script? You a writer?

Pages continue to blow away.

DRIVER. Listen, why don't I just take you uptown. (A writer, you must have lots of things inside of yourself, *stories*.)

CLIFFORD. I need this delivered. I don't want to talk.

DRIVER. I'll take you uptown. Do I have a green light?

CLIFFORD. I'm sorry?

DRIVER. Do I have a green / light?

CLIFFORD. Are you mocking me? I'm blind. *Look* at me.

DRIVER. I'm not mocking you.

CLIFFORD. OK.

DRIVER. Were you blind at birth?

CLIFFORD. No.

DRIVER. D'you have a *disease*?

CLIFFORD. I don't want to talk.

DRIVER. So I just / drive?

CLIFFORD. Just drive. Yes.

They drive.

DRIVER. May I ask your name?

CLIFFORD. (Clifford. Clifford Webb.)

DRIVER. You're not *the* Clifford Webb.

CLIFFORD. Yes as a matter of fact yes I am.

DRIVER (*with joy*). Shit! I have Clifford Webb in my taxi. This is an *honor*, Clifford. Hey . . .

CLIFFORD. (Thank you.)

DRIVER. This is a real honor. I wish I could see your face. I hear your name all the time on the radio. Clifford Webb says this. Clifford Webb thinks that. And my wife she watches that show you do on TV.

They drive.

CLIFFORD. What d'you mean 'see my face'?

DRIVER. She says it is so thought / provoking.

CLIFFORD. What d'you mean 'see my face'? Why can't you see my face?

DRIVER. Listen, you don't want to talk to me, Clifford, and I respect that. Would the radio bother you? Are you trying to *think*?

He turns on the radio.

Softly, the Boogie-Woogie heard at the top of Act 3.

CLIFFORD. Am I losing pages?

The pages continue to blow away and tumble across the space.
The DRIVER *clicks his fingers in time with the music.*

DRIVER. Let's try taking a right here.

Blast of horn.

Take it easy my friend. I have Clifford Webb in the back of this cab.

He continues to click. The music grows louder. The pages tumble
through the air. More frequent horn blasts.

CLIFFORD. What d'you mean 'see my face'? Where is this?
  Where are we going?
DRIVER. I've no idea, Clifford. But isn't that one of the joys,
  one of the great joys of this city?

Music up loud.
Lights fade.
Music continues as they go into the dark.

A Nick Hern Book

The Treatment first published in 1993 as a paperback original
by Nick Hern Books Limited, 14 Larden Road, London W3
7ST in association with the Royal Court Theatre, Sloane
Square, London SW1W 8AS

The Treatment copyright © 1993 by Martin Crimp
Set in Baskerville by ◿ Tek-Art, Addiscombe, Croydon, Surrey
Printed by Cox and Wyman Ltd, Reading, Berks

The right of Martin Crimp to be identified as the author of this
work hs been asserted by him in accordance with the Copyright,
Designs and Patents Act, 1988

A CIP catalogue record for this book is available from the
British Library.

ISBN 1-85459-240-8